BLOCKING,
UNBLOCKING
AND SAFETY
PLAYS IN BRIDGE

Other books by Terence Reese and Roger Trézel
published by Houghton Mifflin Company

The Mistakes You Make at Bridge

BLOCKING, UNBLOCKING AND SAFETY PLAYS IN BRIDGE

Terence Reese and Roger Trézel

A Master Bridge Series title
in conjunction with Peter Crawley

Houghton Mifflin Company

Boston   New York

1993

For information about permission to reproduce selections from
this book, write to Permissions, Houghton Mifflin Company,
215 Park Avenue South, New York, New York 10003.

Library of Congress Cataloguing-in-Publication Data
Reese, Terence.
[Blocking and unblocking plays in bridge]
Blocking, unblocking and safety plays in bridge / Terence Reese and
Roger Trézel.
p. cm.
Originally published in two vols.: Blocking and unblocking plays in bridge.
London : Ward Lock, 1976 and Safety plays in bridge. New York : F. Fell
Publishers, c1976.
"A Master bridge series title in conjunction with Peter Crawley."
ISBN: 0-395-65669-9
1. Contract bridge. I. Trézel, Roger. II. Reese, Terence. Safety plays in
bridge. 1993. III. Title. IV. Series: Master bridge series.
GV1282.3.R3338
795.41'53 — dc20   92-35310
                         CIP

Printed in the United States of America
BP 10 9 8 7 6 5 4 3 2 1

Introduction

by Terence Reese

The play of the cards at bridge is a big subject, capable of filling many large books. Some years ago Roger Trézel, the great French player and writer, had the idea of breaking up the game into several books of the present length, each dealing with one of the standard forms of technique. He judged, quite rightly as it turned out, that this scheme would appeal both to comparative beginners, who would be able to learn the game by stages, and to experienced players wishing to extend their knowledge of a particular branch of play.

We have now worked together on an English version, profiting from his experience.

Blocking and Unblocking Plays

Our aim in this little book is to explain, with the aid of numerous examples, how to overcome those situations where the run of a suit is liable to be blocked. At the same time we describe the more difficult art of blocking an opponent's suit so that he cannot run the tricks that he has on top.

The problem in these blocking and unblocking plays is to perceive in good time how the play is likely to develop. The plays are easy to execute, but to anticipate the need for them is a good deal more tricky.

When you have studied the examples that follow you will be so familiar with plays of this kind that you will easily recognize them in advance and bring them off at the table.

Example 1

As soon as the opening lead has been made, it is essential, before playing any card from dummy, to consider whether any special play is called for in the suit led. Here you are South, playing a contract of three no trumps.

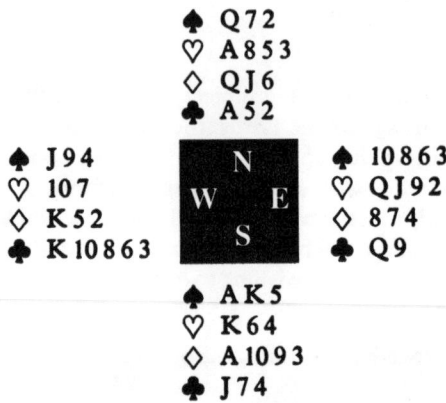

West leads the six of clubs and South, before playing from dummy, counts his top tricks—three spades, two hearts, one diamond and one club. It is easy to establish two more tricks in diamonds, but this involves taking a finesse towards West, who may be able to take four tricks in clubs.

This is precisely what will happen if South makes the mistake of playing a low club from dummy. East will win with the queen and return the nine. If South plays low on this trick West will cover with the ten and force out the ace. When West comes in with the king of diamonds, he will cash his remaining club winners to defeat the contract.

But what will happen if, instead, declarer goes up with the ace of clubs on the opening lead? East will play the nine (it would not help him to unblock) and when West comes in with the king of diamonds either the clubs will be 4—3 or, as in the present case, the run of the suit will be blocked.

It is true that this play of the ace of clubs would cost the contract if West had led from K Q x x x in clubs. But it is more likely that the honours will be divided, and there is the further point that from K Q 10 x x, and probably from K Q 9 x x, West would have led the king, and from K 10 9 x x the 10. Thus the play of the ace will turn out a miscalculation only if West holds precisely K Q 8 6 x.

Example 2

When there is only one division of the cards that will allow you to make your contract, be sure that you profit when this distribution in fact exists. Here you are South, playing in a contract of five diamonds.

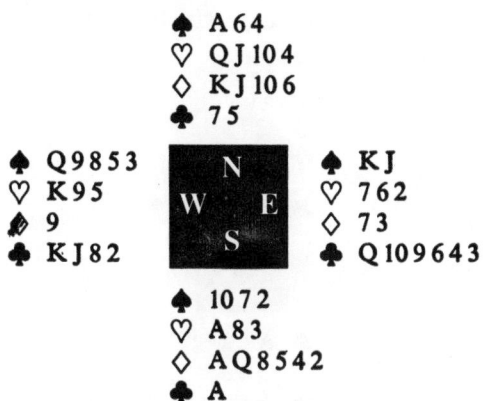

```
            ♠ A 6 4
            ♡ Q J 10 4
            ◇ K J 10 6
            ♣ 7 5
♠ Q 9 8 5 3              ♠ K J
♡ K 9 5       N         ♡ 7 6 2
◇ 9       W     E       ◇ 7 3
♣ K J 8 2     S         ♣ Q 10 9 6 4 3
            ♠ 10 7 2
            ♡ A 8 3
            ◇ A Q 8 5 4 2
            ♣ A
```

West leads the five of spades and South notes unhappily that this is the only lead to create a problem. Against any other lead he would be able to draw trumps, knock out the king of hearts, and discard a spade from his own hand on dummy's fourth heart. But the spade lead appears to give the defenders the 'tempo'. The danger now is that West will hold the king of hearts and will cash the queen of spades when he comes in.

This, indeed, is what will happen if South plays a low spade from dummy at trick one. East will win with the king of spades and return the jack, forcing dummy's ace.

Since the contract would always be safe if the heart finesse were right, South begins by assuming that it is wrong. On that assumption, the only real chance is to find East with two spade honours. Taking advantage of this possibility, South goes up with the ace of spades immediately, draws trumps, and runs the queen of hearts, losing to West's king. Now the spades are blocked and South can dispose of a losing spade on the fourth round of hearts.

It may seem that this play of the ace of spades would be a mistake if East held a singleton honour—presumably the queen, because West would have led an honour from a long suit headed by K Q or Q J. However, with K J 9 8 x x of spades and the king of hearts West might well have entered the bidding.

Example 3

The next deal illustrates a situation that often occurs and is constantly mishandled by average players. It deserves special attention on that account.

You are South, playing three no trumps with these cards:

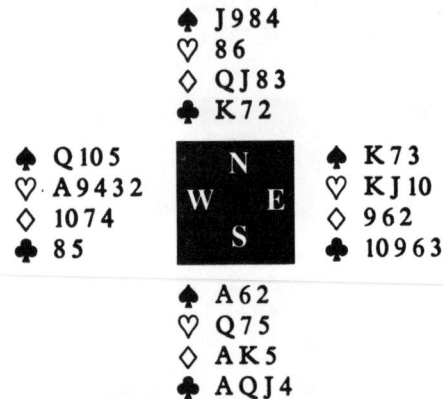

West leads the three of hearts; East goes up with the king and returns the jack. Should South cover with the queen, or not?

It is easy to see that on this occasion the winning play is to cover. If West then plays the ace, the suit will be blocked, and if West holds off, South will easily run the tricks needed for game.

However, most players in this situation would allow the jack to hold. They would argue that there was a better chance to find East with K J alone than with precisely K J 10.

The clue here lies in the opening lead. West's three of hearts, assuming that he follows the normal practice of leading fourth best from a long suit, does not suggest a six-card suit. On the contrary, just as the two can be fourth best only from a suit of four cards, so the three can be fourth best only from four or five cards. It is logical, therefore, to assume that the hearts are divided 5—3, and in that case the best chance is to cover the jack with the queen and hope that this will block the run of the suit.

It is clear that in situations of this kind it is important to study the rank of the card led. It is not, as a rule, difficult to draw the right conclusion against opponents who habitually lead fourth best. We are not tilting against this convention, but certainly there are times when it is more helpful to the declarer than to the defending side.

Example 4

There is one type of position where it is quite easy to block the run of a suit, provided always that you recognize that the opportunity exists. Here you are South, playing three no trumps.

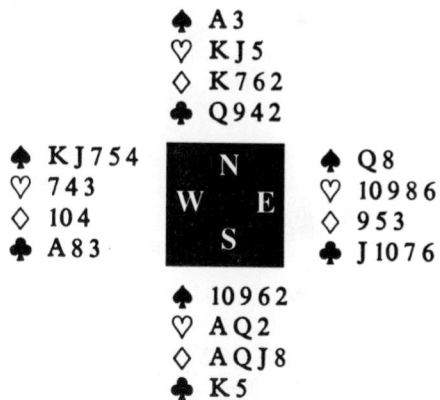

West leads the five of spades. Counting his top tricks, declarer sees four diamonds, three hearts and one spade. The ninth trick can readily be established in clubs, but there is a danger meanwhile that the defence may take four spades and the ace of clubs.

Examining the position more closely, South observes that he will be in no danger if the spades are 4—3, because in that case he will lose at most three spades and the side ace. Nor would there be any danger in a 6—1 division, with East holding a singleton honour.

South must concentrate, therefore, on the possibility of finding the spades 5—2. In this case East will surely hold K x, Q x, or J x, because with K Q J x x West would have led the king.

To play a low spade from dummy at trick one would give opponents the chance to establish four tricks in spades. The right play is to go up with the ace. Now, if East unblocks the queen, South's 10 9 6 will constitute a second stopper, and if East plays low the run of the suit will be blocked.

This is another position of the same kind:

A J

K 10 x x x   Q x

9 8 x x

When West leads a low card it is correct to play the ace from dummy. West would not have led low from K Q 10 x x, so East must hold one of the high cards; whichever it is, after the play of the ace the run of the suit (for four quick tricks) will be effectively blocked.

Example 5

In the examples so far West has made the opening lead from what is presumed to be a long suit. We turn now to a common and critical situation that arises when West leads a suit that has been bid by his partner.

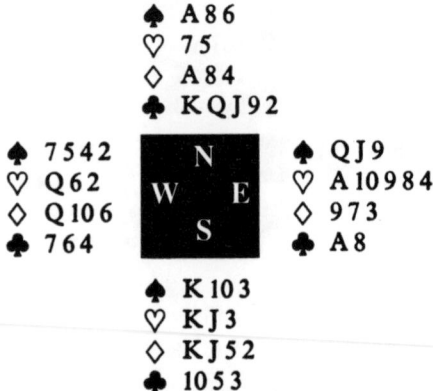

```
                    ♠ A86
                    ♡ 75
                    ◇ A84
                    ♣ KQJ92
    ♠ 7542         N          ♠ QJ9
    ♡ Q62      W       E      ♡ A10984
    ◇ Q106         S          ◇ 973
    ♣ 764                     ♣ A8
                    ♠ K103
                    ♡ KJ3
                    ◇ KJ52
                    ♣ 1053
```

You are South and the bidding has been:

SOUTH	WEST	NORTH	EAST
—	—	1♣	1♡
2 NT	pass	3 NT	pass
pass	pass		

West leads the two of hearts; East goes up with the ace and returns the ten. Which card do you play from hand, the king or the jack?

It may seem natural (if you have not looked at the opposing cards) to finesse the jack, playing East for A Q. But West has led the two, remember, suggesting three to an honour. And since East has returned the ten, the most likely holding for West is Q x x. (It is, of course, correct to lead low from this holding; the lead of the queen would automatically give South a double guard.) Having reached that conclusion, South must go up with the king of hearts. When East comes in with the ace of clubs the run of the hearts suit is blocked.

It is worth remarking that East's return of the ten of hearts is not his best play. He does better to return the eight or nine. South will then have a genuine guess—whether to play West for Q x x or for 10 x x (as from 10 x x also it is correct to lead low in partner's suit).

Here is another situation of the same kind:

$$x$$
$$Jxx \qquad AKxxx$$
$$Q\,10\,xx$$

East has opened the bidding in the suit shown. West leads low to the king and East returns a low card. Now if South plays the ten, the suit will be cleared and East will have tricks to run as soon as he obtains the lead. Declarer's best play at trick two is to go up with the queen. Then he drives out East's card of entry and the main suit is blocked.

Example 6

Never play a card automatically. Always look ahead and consider what is likely to happen. This salutary advice will help you to make the right play on a hand such as the following:

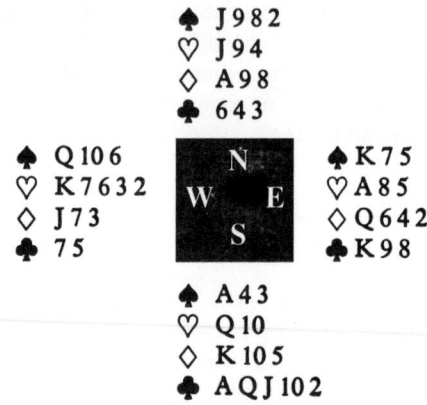

You are South, playing in three no trumps. West leads the three of hearts and East plays the ace. Beware lest, with less than your full attention on the game, you drop the ten!

It is easy to foresee the consequence. East will return the eight of hearts, and when your queen appears, West will naturally hold off, hoping that his partner will have an entry card and a third heart to lead. In with the queen of hearts, you lead a diamond to the ace and take a club finesse, which holds; but you have no second entry to the table, and when the ace of clubs fails to drop the king there will be no play for the contract.

All you need to do on this hand is unblock the hearts by dropping the queen under the ace. If West, as before, holds off the next heart you can overtake the ten with the jack and finesse twice in clubs. Alternatively, West may take the king of hearts and look for tricks in another suit, but you can withstand attack in either spades or diamonds and meanwhile the hearts have not been established.

Example 7

When an opponent's lead against no trumps presents you with a free finesse you will generally gain a trick by accepting the offer. But not always; it is advisable to study the entry position in case, by accepting the free gift of one trick, you deprive yourself of two or more in another suit.

$$
\begin{array}{c}
\spadesuit \ A\,3 \\
\heartsuit \ A\,K \\
\diamondsuit \ A\,64 \\
\clubsuit \ A\,K\,7432
\end{array}
$$

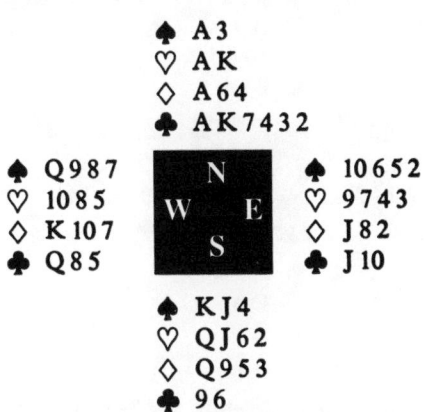

$$
\begin{array}{ll}
\spadesuit \ Q\,987 & \spadesuit \ 10\,652 \\
\heartsuit \ 10\,85 & \heartsuit \ 9743 \\
\diamondsuit \ K\,107 & \diamondsuit \ J\,82 \\
\clubsuit \ Q\,85 & \clubsuit \ J\,10
\end{array}
$$

$$
\begin{array}{c}
\spadesuit \ K\,J\,4 \\
\heartsuit \ Q\,J\,62 \\
\diamondsuit \ Q\,953 \\
\clubsuit \ 96
\end{array}
$$

North opens two clubs (conventional) and South, with his smattering of high cards, responds two no trumps. North bids three clubs and South three diamonds. North then terminates the proceedings with a jump to six no trumps.

West, having an awkward choice, leads the seven of spades. South can let this run to the K J 4, but would this be wise?

It is not such a simple question. South expects the contract to hinge on the club suit, and if clubs are 3—2 he can ensure the contract by going up with the ace of spades, cashing the ace and king of hearts, and clearing the clubs. This will produce five club tricks, four hearts, two spades and one diamond.

But suppose the clubs are 4—1? In that case South may be glad of the extra trick in spades. Let's examine the prospects. South wins the first trick with the jack of spades, cashes the ace of spades, the ace and king of hearts, then leads a low diamond. If East holds K x x of diamonds—and if he makes the mistake of going up with the king—declarer will have twelve tricks. But it is easy to see that this is a much poorer chance than playing for a 3—2 break in clubs.

Thus the correct play, undoubtedly, is to decline the free offer presented by the spade lead. South must go up with the ace of spades and be careful to unblock the ace and king of hearts before clearing the clubs. If he fails to do this the defenders may drive out the spade entry before South can enjoy the queen and jack of hearts.

Example 8

When the dummy is short of entries it is often necessary to unblock from hand to prepare for a finesse that will win an extra trick. Two examples follow, where declarer must unblock a doubleton queen.

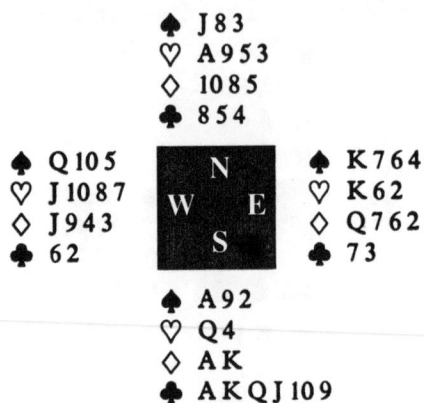

```
                ♠ J 8 3
                ♡ A 9 5 3
                ◇ 10 8 5
                ♣ 8 5 4

♠ Q 10 5         N          ♠ K 7 6 4
♡ J 10 8 7                  ♡ K 6 2
◇ J 9 4 3     W     E       ◇ Q 7 6 2
♣ 6 2            S          ♣ 7 3

                ♠ A 9 2
                ♡ Q 4
                ◇ A K
                ♣ A K Q J 10 9
```

South opens with a conventional two clubs and North responds two hearts, showing the ace.* South bids three clubs and North signs off in three no trumps. No doubt South should pass this, but as an ace and a king would put him in the slam zone he tests the weather with four no trumps, Blackwood, asking for kings. North denies a king with five clubs and South passes, content that (a) he will score 150 for honours and (b) he will be playing it.

West leads the jack of hearts, dummy plays low, and East goes up with the king. South has the opportunity now to retrieve his reputation by unblocking with the queen. So long as he does this he can later finesse the nine of hearts, for a spade discard on the ace of hearts. If he fails to unblock, he will never be able to enter dummy to cash the ace and will be reduced to the slender hope of dropping a doubleton K Q of spades or of finding East with a singleton king or queen of spades.

---

*This is the French style, followed also in the CAB system. I must say that I am strongly opposed to it ! T.R.

Example 9

The declarer has to make the same kind of play—unblocking a queen—on the next hand, but the circumstances are a little different.

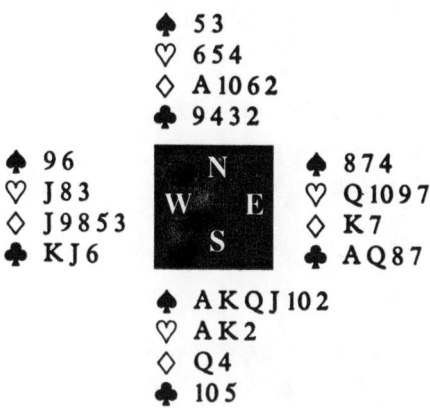

```
              ♠ 5 3
              ♡ 6 5 4
              ◇ A 10 6 2
              ♣ 9 4 3 2
♠ 9 6              N              ♠ 8 7 4
♡ J 8 3        W     E          ♡ Q 10 9 7
◇ J 9 8 5 3       S              ◇ K 7
♣ K J 6                          ♣ A Q 8 7
              ♠ A K Q J 10 2
              ♡ A K 2
              ◇ Q 4
              ♣ 10 5
```

South opens two spades, forcing for one round, his partner responds two no trumps, and South bids three spades. Holding an ace, but with only one suit guarded, North raises to four spades. It may be observed that once again the nine-trick contract of three no trumps would have been a better proposition. It fails only if clubs are 5—2, and the suit is not blocked, (as would happen, for example, if West led the king from K Q J x x and his partner held A x).

West leads the five of diamonds, dummy plays low and East the king. South's only chance of making two tricks in diamonds is to unblock the queen. If the defenders play on clubs, attempting to cash three tricks in this suit, South will ruff, draw trumps, and make his contract by finessing the ten of diamonds and discarding his losing heart on the ace of diamonds.

Can the defence prevent this in any way ? Yes, by the pretty and imaginative play of returning a diamond at once (or after two rounds of clubs). When dummy attempts to cash the ace of diamonds East will ruff and South will be left with four losers.

Note that South is defeated only because the diamonds are 5—2 and the defence has played well. If diamonds were 4—3, West holding the jack, the unblock of the queen would always win the contract.

Note, also, that if diamonds are not played early on, South will always succeed. After drawing the trumps he will lead the queen of diamonds and let it run. East will win and a finesse of the ten will follow. And if the queen of diamonds is covered by the king ? In that case, again, South must play low from dummy, hoping that West began with K J x or K J x x. The critical card, always, is the jack of diamonds.

Example 10

There were several ways of playing the next deal. South chose a
reasonable line but made a calamitous error at the finish.

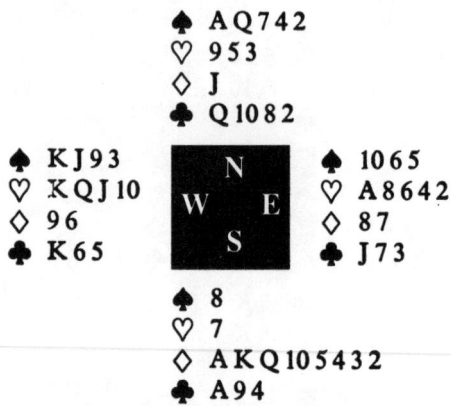

♠ A Q 7 4 2
♡ 9 5 3
◇ J
♣ Q 10 8 2

♠ K J 9 3
♡ K Q J 10
◇ 9 6
♣ K 6 5

♠ 10 6 5
♡ A 8 6 4 2
◇ 8 7
♣ J 7 3

♠ 8
♡ 7
◇ A K Q 10 5 4 3 2
♣ A 9 4

South was in five diamonds and the defence began with two rounds
of hearts. South's problem was to avoid losing two club tricks. There
was something to be said for drawing trumps and leading a low club to the
ten (or the queen). If this finesse lost, East would not be able to return a
spade and South could try for the drop of the outstanding club honour,
with the spade finesse in reserve. But the most favoured way to play
this club combination is to lead twice from the Q 10 8 x, and with this
intention in mind South crossed to the jack of diamonds and led the
queen of clubs, losing to West's king.

West exited with a third heart and South then ran off the trumps, arriving at this position:

A possible line of play now would be to lay down the ace of clubs and then lead the last trump. This would gain if the jack of clubs fell; if West held king of spades and jack of clubs he would have an impossible discard; and if East held those two cards he would have to bare the king of spades. Whatever happened, the spade finesse would be available.

However, South had another idea. He played off the last trump and threw the eight of clubs from dummy. Then he led a spade to the ace and played the ten of clubs from the table. But of course East did not cover and South had to lose the last trick. It was impossible, really, to lose five diamonds on this deal, but South found a way—through failing to unblock dummy's ten of clubs in preparation for a finesse.

Example 11

The next deal has the appearance of an old-fashioned double dummy problem. It shows in striking fashion how a lack of communication can sometimes be overcome.

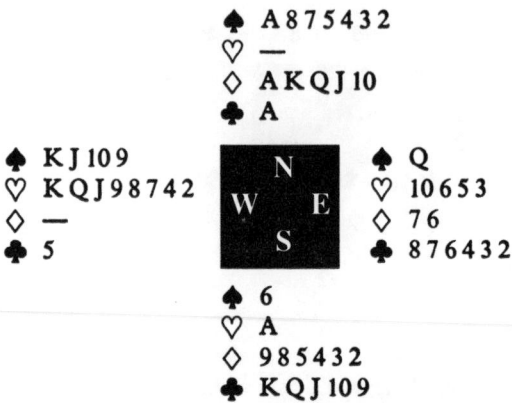

```
              ♠ A 8 7 5 4 3 2
              ♡ —
              ◇ A K Q J 10
              ♣ A
  ♠ K J 10 9              ♠ Q
  ♡ K Q J 9 8 7 4 2       ♡ 10 6 5 3
  ◇ —                     ◇ 7 6
  ♣ 5                     ♣ 8 7 6 4 3 2
              ♠ 6
              ♡ A
              ◇ 9 8 5 4 3 2
              ♣ K Q J 10 9
```

North is the dealer and North-South are vulnerable. North-South are playing the forcing two system and the bidding goes:

SOUTH	WEST	NORTH	EAST
—	—	2♠	pass
3◇	4♡	6◇	6♡
pass	(1) pass	7◇	pass
pass	7♡	dble	pass
7 NT	(2) pass	pass	pass

1) South passes to show that he controls the hearts and is not hostile to the idea of playing in seven diamonds.

2) After his partner has bid seven diamonds South expects the diamonds to be solid. He is not going to be deprived of the chance for a vulnerable grand slam.

Seven no trumps cannot be made on a spade or club lead, but West quite naturally leads the king of hearts. Quite easy now! South discards the ace of clubs on the first trick. Five top diamonds go away on the K Q J 10 9 of clubs; and then six spades on the 9 8 5 4 3 2 of diamonds!

You may never play a hand quite so spectacular as this, but you see the idea?

Example 12

'Take care of the pence and the pounds will look after themselves'
may have been a sound (pre-inflation) maxim, but at bridge the opposite
situation exists. Small economies can lead to large losses.

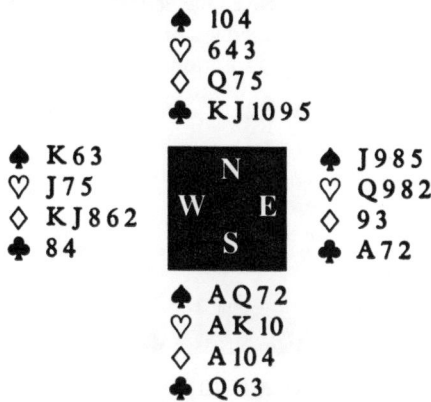

```
              ♠ 10 4
              ♡ 6 4 3
              ◇ Q 7 5
              ♣ K J 10 9 5
♠ K 6 3                        ♠ J 9 8 5
♡ J 7 5          N             ♡ Q 9 8 2
◇ K J 8 6 2    W   E           ◇ 9 3
♣ 8 4             S            ♣ A 7 2
              ♠ A Q 7 2
              ♡ A K 10
              ◇ A 10 4
              ♣ Q 6 3
```

Stretching a little, South opens two no trumps and North raises to three
no trumps. West leads the six of diamonds, dummy plays low, East plays
the nine and South wins with the ten.

Declarer plays two rounds of clubs, but the opponents meanly hold up
the ace. (West plays the eight on the first round, playing high-low to
indicate a doubleton.) When East takes the third round of clubs he leads
a diamond and South ends up with seven tricks.

'Sorry, partner, I didn't quite have my bid.'

But it was the play that let him down, not the bidding. West's lead of
the six of diamonds was presumably fourth best. Applying the rule of
eleven (subtracting the rank of the card led from eleven), South could
judge that West held the remaining high diamonds, including the king.
It was essential to retain an entry to dummy, in case the ace of clubs
could not be driven out on the first two rounds. At trick one, therefore,
South must capture the nine of diamonds with the ace, not the ten.
He forces out the ace of clubs, and the difference is that the queen of
diamonds is a sure entry to the table. South makes game with four
clubs, two diamonds, two hearts and a spade.

Note that South's economy in winning the first trick with the ten of
diamonds did not even gain a trick in diamonds. Assuming that West
held the king, there were always two tricks in diamonds, no more and
no less.

Example 13

Sometimes no amount of unblocking within a single suit will enable the declarer to run all the tricks that should legitimately be his. Look at the club suit below. If the jack falls in two rounds, there is no problem in taking five tricks, but if the jack is twice guarded, there is no way to run all the tricks, because South has no card lower than dummy's five and three. There is nevertheless a pretty solution.

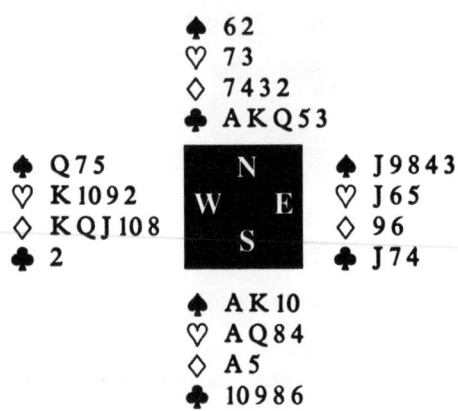

South is in three no trumps and West leads the king of diamonds. Not fearing a switch to any other suit, South holds off. West plays another diamond, which is taken by the ace.

South leads the eight of clubs to the queen and follows with a second round, on which West discards a heart. If the clubs had been 2—2, South could have returned to the ten and made the last two clubs in dummy, but now the suit is blocked.

Declarer may seek his ninth trick by way of a finesse in hearts, but this is only a 50% chance—slightly better, perhaps, after West has turned up with a good suit of diamonds. However, there is a much surer way. In dummy after two rounds of clubs, South leads a diamond and discards a club from his own hand. West runs his diamond winners, but with only one club left in hand, and K 5 3 on the table, South can make game with five clubs and four top winners in the other suits.

Sometimes there is a slight risk in this form of play, but there was none here. East had already been seen to follow to two rounds of diamonds, so West could have five at most; there was no danger of his cashing enough tricks to beat the contract.

Example 14

The unblocking play required on the deal below is similar in type to some of those shown earlier (Examples 8 and 9), but the play is easier to miss.

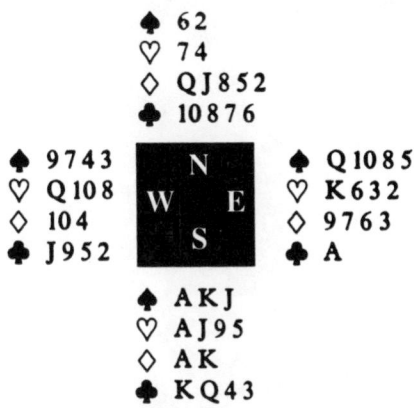

♠ 6 2
♡ 7 4
◇ Q J 8 5 2
♣ 10 8 7 6

♠ 9 7 4 3
♡ Q 10 8
◇ 10 4
♣ J 9 5 2

♠ Q 10 8 5
♡ K 6 3 2
◇ 9 7 6 3
♣ A

♠ A K J
♡ A J 9 5
◇ A K
♣ K Q 4 3

South opens with a conventional two clubs and North responds two diamonds. Most players would tot up their 25 points and bid three no trumps, although this hand would not make a game with a blank hand opposite. However, if South bids only a cautious two no trumps, North has enough to raise to three.

West leads the two of clubs to the six, ace and three. East will probably return a spade and . . .

Ah! You wanted to ask why South had not unblocked the queen of clubs on the first lead ?

Quite so. If South plays a low club on the first trick, he will make only eight tricks—two clubs, two diamonds, a heart, and three spades (because sooner or later the opponents will be forced to give him a chance to finesse the jack).

To make the contract, South must unblock the clubs at trick one to create an entry to dummy. East's best return, as the cards lie, is a heart. South puts in the nine and West wins with the ten. West will probably continue with the queen of hearts. South can afford to take this ; then he cashes the ace and king of diamonds and follows with the king and another club. The defenders make two clubs and two hearts, but that is all.

Note that, as in the earlier example, the unblock of the queen of clubs does not even cost a trick in clubs.

Example 15

The next deal bears a cousinly relationship to Example 12. We make no apology for giving a second hand on the same theme, especially as this one contains two additional points of interest.

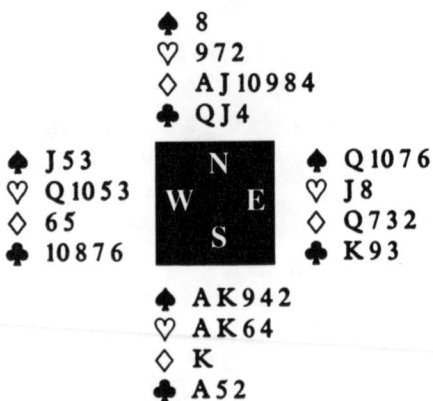

```
              ♠ 8
              ♡ 9 7 2
              ◇ A J 10 9 8 4
              ♣ Q J 4
  ♠ J 5 3          N          ♠ Q 10 7 6
  ♡ Q 10 5 3    W     E       ♡ J 8
  ◇ 6 5             S          ◇ Q 7 3 2
  ♣ 10 8 7 6                  ♣ K 9 3
              ♠ A K 9 4 2
              ♡ A K 6 4
              ◇ K
              ♣ A 5 2
```

South plays in three no trumps and West leads the six of clubs. It is tempting, perhaps, to go up with the queen of clubs in dummy. This play would not be costly if East made the mistake of covering with the king, but a good player in East's position would be conscious of the need to prevent the jack of clubs from becoming an entry card. East plays low on the queen of clubs, therefore. South may attempt to retrieve his error by overtaking with the ace, but when he seeks to enter dummy later with the jack of clubs he will be disappointed.

The correct play, making sure of an entry to dummy, is to play the four of clubs on the first trick and win with the ace. Then the diamonds are unblocked by overtaking the king with the ace and forcing out the queen. With the Q J of clubs providing an entry, South will have no difficulty in making eleven tricks.

Example 16

One of the most satisfactory forms of play consists of forcing an opponent to provide an entry to tricks that seem to be out of reach. Observe the declarer's management of his four-heart contract on the following deal:

With a little more trust in his partner—or a little less fondness for his 100 honours—South could have let North play three no trumps, but instead he battled his way to four hearts.

The play began inauspiciously when West led the queen of clubs to his partner's ace. East returned the jack, the king was ruffed, and West exited with a heart. South drew trumps, cashed the ace of diamonds, then played the ace of spades and jack of spades, overtaking with the queen. The position was:

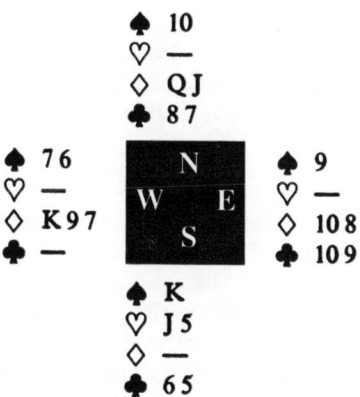

South led the queen of diamonds from dummy and discarded his obstructing king of spades. West was compelled to give dummy the lead in either spades or diamonds, enabling South to discard his two club losers.

Example 17

We saw an example earlier (12) where a declarer whose suit was liable
to be blocked contrived to dispose of an unwanted card. The method he
adopted then was to lead a loser from dummy and discard from his own
hand. On this next deal the defenders, in all probability, will give South
the opportunity to discard on a winner.

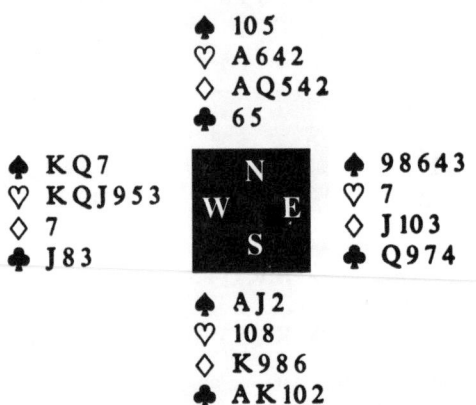

♠ 10 5
♡ A 6 4 2
◇ A Q 5 4 2
♣ 6 5

♠ K Q 7
♡ K Q J 9 5 3
◇ 7
♣ J 8 3

♠ 9 8 6 4 3
♡ 7
◇ J 10 3
♣ Q 9 7 4

♠ A J 2
♡ 10 8
◇ K 9 8 6
♣ A K 10 2

North-South are vulnerable and South opens one no trump. West
intervenes with two hearts. North has enough to double, but he prefers to
play for a vulnerable game and raises to three no trumps.

West leads the king of hearts and South, counting his tricks, sees one in
spades, one in hearts, two in clubs and, probably, five in diamonds. But
there's a snag. Suppose the diamonds are 3—1: in that case the run of
the suit will be blocked.

Fortunately, there is a simple remedy. Declarer must not take either the
first or second round of hearts. On the third round he goes up with the ace
in dummy and discards an obstructive diamond. Five diamond tricks are
then available whether the suit is 3—1 or 2—2.

It is possible, though not at all likely, that West will abandon the hearts
after the first or second trick. But that creates no serious problem. If West
takes two hearts, then switches to the king of spades, the ace of hearts will
still be available for the discard of a diamond. And if West switches after
just one round of hearts, declarer wins with the ace of spades and plays
king and ace of diamonds. Discovering the 3—1 break, he exits from
dummy with a low heart. When next in, he plays a diamond to the queen
and discards his fourth diamond on the ace of hearts.

Example 18

Every bid made by an opponent (and every failure to bid, for that matter) provides some indication about the lie of the cards. Even when the overcall seems not to affect the play, it is important to take note of any clue to the distribution.

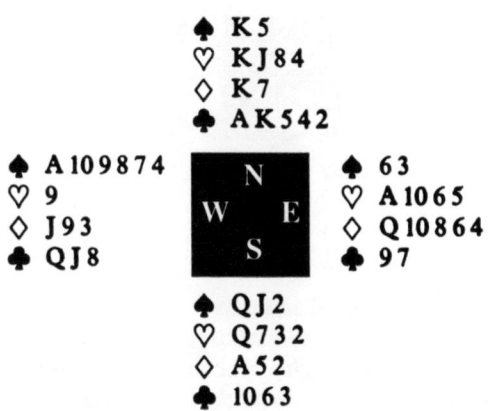

```
              ♠ K 5
              ♡ K J 8 4
              ◇ K 7
              ♣ A K 5 4 2
♠ A 10 9 8 7 4              ♠ 6 3
♡ 9            N           ♡ A 10 6 5
◇ J 9 3    W     E         ◇ Q 10 8 6 4
♣ Q J 8       S            ♣ 9 7
              ♠ Q J 2
              ♡ Q 7 3 2
              ◇ A 5 2
              ♣ 10 6 3
```

North opens one club, South responds one heart, and West comes in with two spades. North raises to three hearts and South bids the game.

Against four hearts, West leads the ace of spades. Before playing from dummy, South must consider where he wants the lead to be at trick two. He has certain losers in clubs and spades and must avoid losing two trump tricks. As West has overcalled and is therefore marked with length in spades, East is more likely than West to hold four hearts. As West might hold a singleton ace, it could be a mistake to lead a heart honour from dummy. South makes his first good play, therefore, by unblocking dummy's king of spades.

West might consider switching to a diamond, playing his partner from A Q of diamonds and a trump trick. That is a remote chance, however, and we will say that West continues with a second spade, taken by the queen.

A low heart goes to the king and ace, and East exits with a diamond which goes to dummy's king. On the jack of hearts West discards a spade.

The position is now:

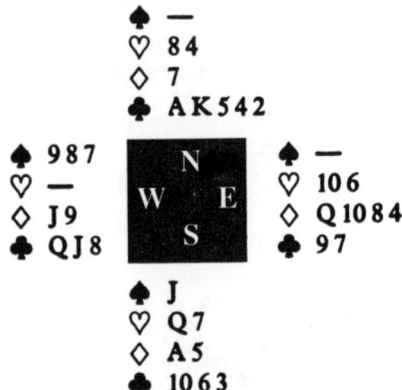

South must take care of his third diamond, so he plays a diamond to the ace and returns the five. He must be sure to ruff with dummy's eight of hearts at this point, so that he can play back the four and pick up East's 10 6. Suppose, instead, that he ruffs with the four of hearts and returns the eight. East will not cover, so the eight wins; but then West will win the third round of clubs and play a spade, enabling East to make his ten of hearts and defeat the contract.

Example 19

Sometimes a bad division of the trumps, combined with a lack of communication, will necessitate an unblock. The play may be quite simple when the need for it appears, but it may also require some foresight.

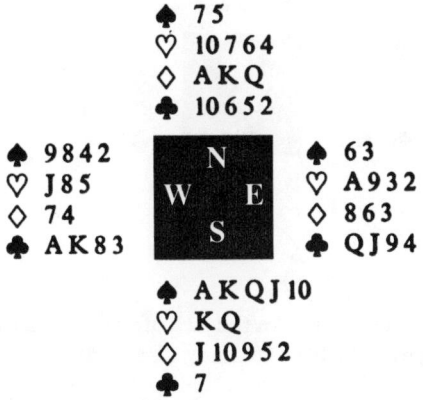

South plays in four spades and the defence begins with two rounds of clubs, forcing declarer to ruff.

In a sense there are ten tricks on top—five diamonds and five spades—but there is an unpleasant block in the diamond suit and South has been reduced already to four trumps. Suppose he begins by playing off three top trumps, hoping for a 3—3 break. When East shows out, South's best chance is to play off dummy's ace and king of diamonds, then lead a heart from dummy. East must go up with the ace and lead another club. South can ruff with his last trump, but West will still hold a trump and a winning club.

Declarer should see that he may easily lose control and have difficulty in regaining the lead if trumps are 4—2. After ruffing the second club he should plan to unblock in diamonds. The best play is to take one round of diamonds, then run the trumps, discarding high diamonds from the table.

This is the position when the last trump is led:

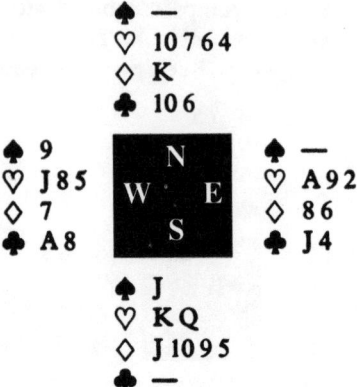

```
              ♠ —
              ♡ 10 7 6 4
              ◇ K
              ♣ 10 6
  ♠ 9              N          ♠ —
  ♡ J 8 5                     ♡ A 9 2
  ◇ 7        W      E         ◇ 8 6
  ♣ A 8          S            ♣ J 4
              ♠ J
              ♡ K Q
              ◇ J 10 9 5
              ♣ —
```

The king of diamonds goes away on the jack of spades and the way is clear then for South to make his remaining diamonds.

Example 20

The deal below contains no fewer than four tests: South must decide which suit to establish in three no trumps; he must make an advance unblocking play; the defender, West, must counter with a blocking play; and finally South must turn to another suit to establish the additional winner he needs.

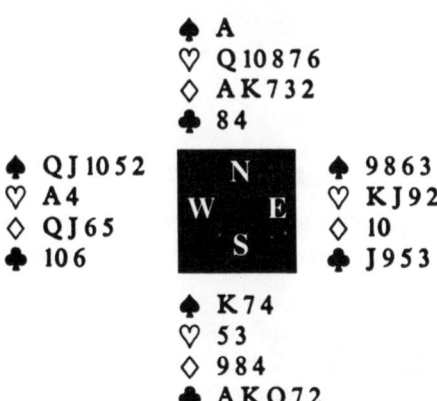

```
                ♠ A
                ♡ Q 10 8 7 6
                ◇ A K 7 3 2
                ♣ 8 4
♠ Q J 10 5 2        N        ♠ 9 8 6 3
♡ A 4          W         E    ♡ K J 9 2
◇ Q J 6 5          S         ◇ 10
♣ 10 6                       ♣ J 9 5 3
                ♠ K 7 4
                ♡ 5 3
                ◇ 9 8 4
                ♣ A K Q 7 2
```

South plays in three no trumps and West leads the queen of spades to dummy's ace.

Declarer has seven tricks on top and his first problem is whether to play on clubs or diamonds for the extra tricks. Players are often told to play on the *longest* suit, but that is not always good advice. For example, if you hold Q J 10 9 opposite x x you dispose of only six cards, but you can be sure of establishing two additional tricks, with little risk. Thus the best general guide is that you should set out to establish the suit that will provide most winners in addition to those already available.

In the present instance diamonds are both the longest suit and the suit where you have the best chance to develop two extra tricks. If clubs are 3—3, this suit can wait; and if clubs are 4—1, you will establish only one long card.

On all grounds, therefore, South should play on diamonds first. He must duck a round of diamonds, as dummy has no side entries after the ace of spades has been driven out. Preparing for a finesse that may be necessary, South plays the ace of diamonds and drops the eight from hand when he sees East's ten. He follows with a low diamond to the nine. It is clear that if West captures this trick, declarer will be able to run three more diamond tricks by leading the four and finessing dummy's seven.

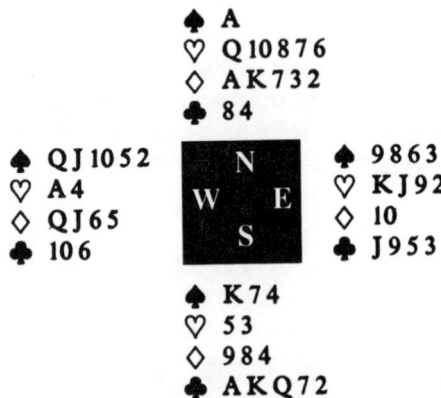

Realizing this, West may decline to win the second diamond. He will retain the Q J so that declarer can make only the king in dummy and no long cards.

As it happens, South can overcome this defence by turning to the clubs. He has made three tricks in diamonds and now needs only four in clubs. The best play is to duck a round of clubs; the defenders will be able to run at most three tricks in hearts, and whatever they play next South will be able to take the four club tricks needed for his contract.

Example 21

You may never, in your entire bridge life, play quite so spectacular a hand as the one below, but the type of unblocking play that it illustrates is by no means unique.

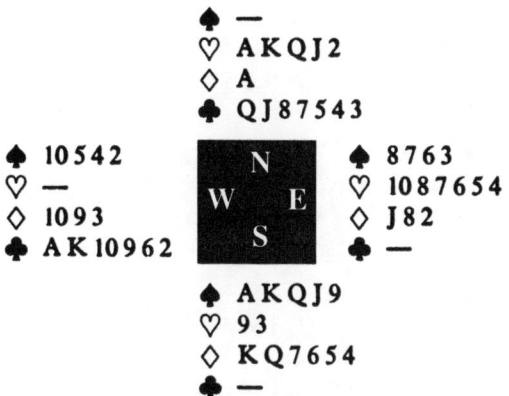

After a fighting auction (the fight being between the partners, North and South) South ends up the 'winner' in a contract of six spades.

On the opening lead of the king of clubs, East discards a heart and South ruffs. For declarer to have a chance, two things must happen: the spades must break 4—4 and the diamonds 3—3. But that is not enough, because after drawing trumps and crossing to the ace of diamonds South will have no re-entry to hand (remember he has already used one of his trumps when ruffing the opening lead). Nor will it help to discard the ace of diamonds on the trump leads, because then there will be a diamond loser.

Oddly enough, if the spades are 4—4 and the diamonds 3—3, South has a sure way to make the contract. East has already shown out on the clubs, so his remaining six cards must all be hearts. On the four trumps South discards four top hearts from the table. Then he crosses to the ace of diamonds and leads a low heart, forcing East to concede an entry to South's 9 x.

You may think that six diamonds would have been a better contract. But this can be beaten. East ruffs the king of clubs with the eight of diamonds. South overruffs, crosses to the ace of diamonds, and leads another club; East ruffs with the jack, promoting two trump tricks for his partner. And if South, when in dummy after the ace of diamonds, plays a heart instead of a club, West will ruff and play a club, again establishing a second trump trick.

Example 22

Beware of false economies when you play this game. Sometimes—we have seen many examples already—it is wiser to discard high cards than low ones.

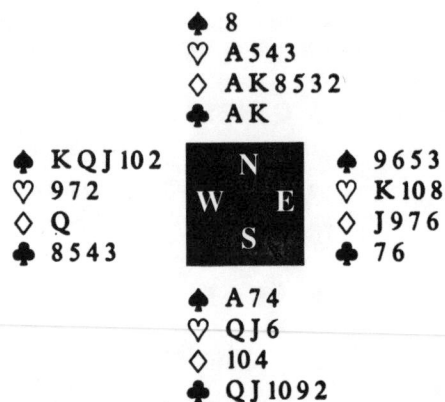

```
                  ♠ 8
                  ♡ A 5 4 3
                  ◇ A K 8 5 3 2
                  ♣ A K
  ♠ K Q J 10 2                    ♠ 9 6 5 3
  ♡ 9 7 2         N              ♡ K 10 8
  ◇ Q          W     E           ◇ J 9 7 6
  ♣ 8 5 4 3        S              ♣ 7 6
                  ♠ A 7 4
                  ♡ Q J 6
                  ◇ 10 4
                  ♣ Q J 10 9 2
```

Playing a two club system in which two-bids are not forcing, North opens two diamonds. South responds two no trumps, North shows his hearts, and South's three no trumps closes the auction.

West leads the king of spades and South ducks. West follows with a second spade and if South is not fully awake at this point he will lose the contract. He must begin to unblock the clubs by throwing the king of clubs from dummy. Now if West leads another spade, South disposes of the second high club while winning in hand with the ace of spades. Then he runs five club tricks and makes game easily.

If South fails to unblock the clubs at trick two he will have no play for the contract. Even if the diamonds were 3—2, the defence would make four spades and a diamond.

An expert West, it is true, having seen the discard of the king of clubs at trick two, would realize what declarer was aiming to do and might switch to a diamond. South can withstand this quite easily. He cashes the remaining high club and forces entry to hand by leading a heart towards the Q J 6.

Example 23

To throw a king under an opponent's ace, when you do not hold the queen, may seem to be unduly theatrical. Nevertheless, such play may be both correct and necessary, as the following example shows.

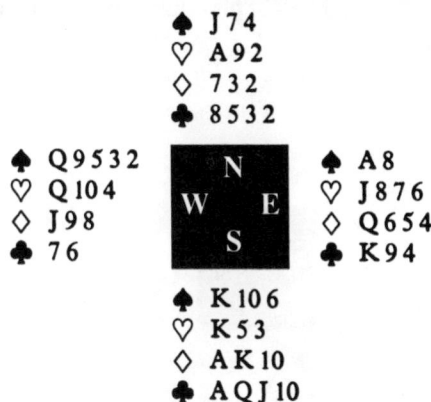

South opens two no trumps and North raises to three no trumps. West leads the three of spades, dummy plays low, and East wins with the ace.

Prospects are not too good. South cannot expect to make more than one trick in spades. There are two in hearts and two in diamonds, so he will need four tricks from clubs. This will not be difficult if East has K x or king alone, but there appears to be only one entry to dummy, the ace of hearts. This being so, declarer will not be able to pick up the king of clubs if it is twice guarded.

However, South can restore the situation by dropping the king of spades under the ace; then the opponents cannot develop the spades without letting dummy in with the jack. If East tries another suit at trick two South can play a spade himself.

Note that the same type of unblock would be necessary if South held Q x x of spades instead of K 10 x. And even with a doubleton K x or Q x it might, in slightly different circumstances, be good play to throw the honour card under the ace.

Example 24

The deal below was used many years ago in a 'par contest'—an event in which the hands are prepared. It was considered difficult and created quite a sensation. But we believe that any reader who has studied the examples up to now will find the right play quite readily, and even without looking at the East-West cards.

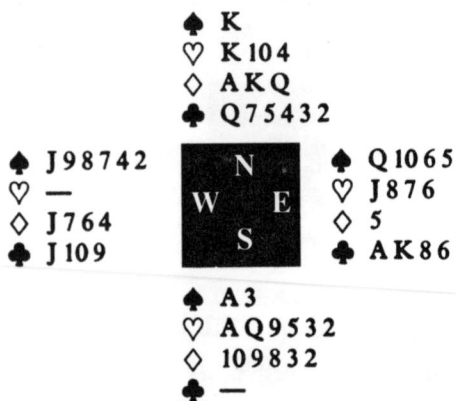

```
                   ♠ K
                   ♡ K 10 4
                   ◇ A K Q
                   ♣ Q 7 5 4 3 2

♠ J 9 8 7 4 2         N          ♠ Q 10 6 5
♡ —              W         E     ♡ J 8 7 6
◇ J 7 6 4                        ◇ 5
♣ J 10 9              S          ♣ A K 8 6

                   ♠ A 3
                   ♡ A Q 9 5 3 2
                   ◇ 10 9 8 3 2
                   ♣ —
```

West leads the jack of clubs against South's contract of six hearts. South ruffs and lays down the ace of hearts, on which West discards a spade.

The first test occurs at this moment. To facilitate the run of the trump suit, declarer must unblock by playing the ten of hearts under the ace. He follows with a heart to the king and lays down the king of spades.

The hand would be quite simple if diamonds were 3—2. South could draw trumps, cash the top diamonds in dummy and make thirteen tricks. But suppose the diamonds are 4—1 ? In that case declarer will be in danger of losing control. Remember that he has ruffed the opening lead, so after drawing East's four trumps he will have only one heart left in his own hand. If the jack of diamonds does not fall under the A K Q, he will never establish his long diamond.

To take care of a 4—1 break in diamonds, South must cash one high diamond when on the table and must manoeuvre to discard the other two.

This is the position after a club ruff, two rounds of trumps, king of spades and ace of diamonds:

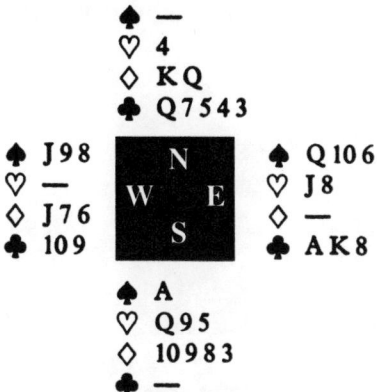

South finesses the nine of hearts, draws the queen, discarding ◊K, and follows with the ace of spades, discarding ◊Q. Then he forces out the jack of diamonds and still has a trump left, which enables him to make the remaining diamonds.

Example 25

When dummy has a side suit but is short of entries, it is often possible to create entries in the trump suit by ruffing with high trumps and using low ones to cross to the dummy.

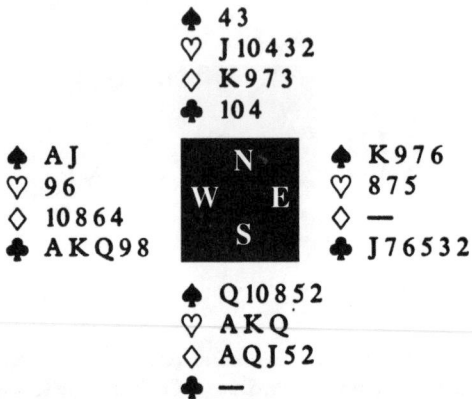

```
              ♠ 43
              ♡ J 10 4 3 2
              ◇ K 9 7 3
              ♣ 10 4

♠ A J                         ♠ K 9 7 6
♡ 9 6            N            ♡ 8 7 5
◇ 10 8 6 4    W   E          ◇ —
♣ A K Q 9 8      S            ♣ J 7 6 5 3 2

              ♠ Q 10 8 5 2
              ♡ A K Q
              ◇ A Q J 5 2
              ♣ —
```

South is the dealer, with East-West vulnerable, and the bidding goes:

SOUTH	WEST	NORTH	EAST
1♠	2♣	pass	3♣
3◇	4♣	4◇	5♣
5◇	dble	pass	pass
pass			

West leads the king of clubs and at first sight the hand looks easy: five trumps, five hearts, and one ruff make up eleven tricks. However, West's double suggests that the diamonds may be 4—0. If that is so, it will not be possible to draw trumps and take a ruff in dummy.

The way to overcome a 4—0 break is to extend the power of the trump suit by taking two ruffs in hand. South must take care meanwhile not to allow the hearts to become blocked.

The first step is to ruff the club lead with a high trump and lay down the ace of diamonds. When East's void is revealed South follows with a low diamond, covering West's card. Then he ruffs a second club with the queen of diamonds, arriving at this position:

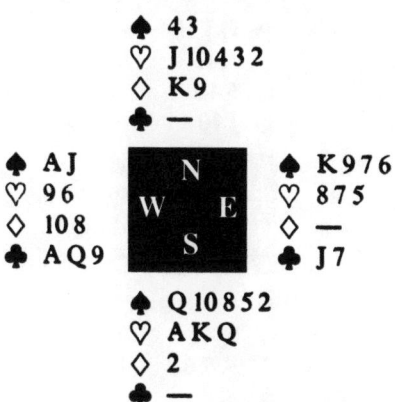

Using a technique that we have observed on some earlier hands, declarer cashes the ace and king of hearts, then finesses the nine of diamonds and discards the queen of hearts on the king of diamonds. That leaves the dummy high except for the two losing spades.

You will find that if South ruffs the opening club lead with a low trump he can never make this contract. The best lead for the defence is a trump, and indeed there is a good case for this.

Example 26

There is an old saying that a singleton king will always make. This may be true in many cases when the singleton is held by a defender, but the declarer's chances of making a singleton king are by no means so good.

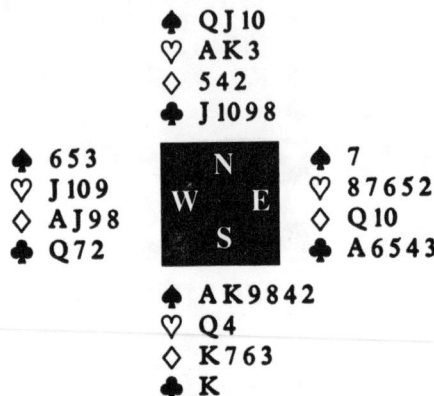

```
              ♠ Q J 10
              ♡ A K 3
              ◇ 5 4 2
              ♣ J 10 9 8
  ♠ 6 5 3         N          ♠ 7
  ♡ J 10 9     W     E       ♡ 8 7 6 5 2
  ◇ A J 9 8       S          ◇ Q 10
  ♣ Q 7 2                    ♣ A 6 5 4 3
              ♠ A K 9 8 4 2
              ♡ Q 4
              ◇ K 7 6 3
              ♣ K
```

South was in four spades and West led the jack of hearts. At the table South formed a rather naive plan: he won in dummy and led the jack of clubs, hoping that East would duck and that he would make his singleton king. However, East went up with the ace of clubs and led the queen of diamonds, establishing three more tricks for the defence.

It would have been better play to take three rounds of hearts, discarding the king of clubs, then play a diamond from dummy. The defenders must be smart enough now to play a trump each time they are in with a diamond; this will prevent South from ruffing the fourth round.

Once three rounds of hearts have stood up, the surest way to win the contract is to lead the jack of clubs from the table and let it run if not covered by East. West wins and leads a trump (or a diamond, which will solve all problems). Dummy wins and plays another club through East's ace; again, if East does not cover, he lets the ten run. Only one club trick is needed for the contract.

When he throws the king of clubs on the third heart, South is not only discarding a loser: he is unblocking the clubs so that he can establish a winner by means of the two ruffing finesses.

Example 27

When is a free finesse not so free ? When it causes the declarer to win in the wrong hand, so depriving him of two tricks in another suit (Example 7); and when it causes him actually to make one trick less than he should in the suit led, as here:

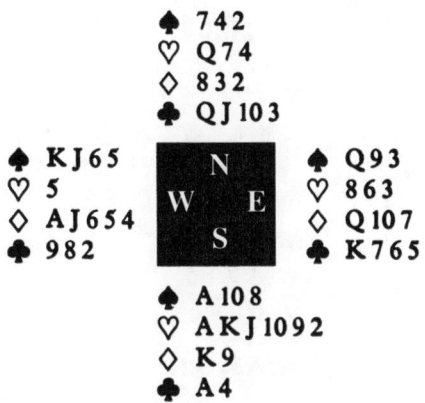

```
              ♠ 742
              ♡ Q74
              ◊ 832
              ♣ QJ103

♠ KJ65         N         ♠ Q93
♡ 5        W       E     ♡ 863
◊ AJ654                  ◊ Q107
♣ 982          S         ♣ K765

              ♠ A108
              ♡ AKJ1092
              ◊ K9
              ♣ A4
```

South plays in four hearts, no other suit having been mentioned. Anxious to protect his tenace holdings in spades and diamonds, West makes the apparently safe lead of the nine of clubs. Happily accepting the offer of a free finesse, declarer goes up with the queen in dummy. East, very properly, declines to contribute the king, so the queen holds the trick.

After a trump to the ace, South realizes that he has been somewhat prodigal in playing the queen of clubs at trick one. Hoping to find the trumps 2—2, he cashes the ace of clubs and leads the ten of hearts to the queen. Unfortunately, the hearts do not break. It is no use leading the jack of clubs now, because East will cover and there will be no entry to the table. The best that declarer can do is lead a diamond to the king; this loses to the ace, and eventually South loses two diamonds and two spades.

Once he has escaped a spade lead, which as the cards lie would always beat the contract, South has only to avoid blocking the clubs to make ten tricks. He must play low from dummy at trick one and win with the ace. After two high trumps he leads a club to the ten and king. Now the queen of hearts is an entry for two more club tricks.

Example 28

The next hand is rather difficult. You may nevertheless find the solution if you recall the theme of a previous deal. (We will not, for the moment, tell you which.)

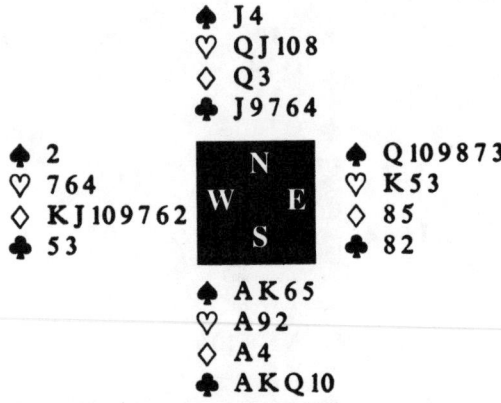

South opens with a conventional two clubs and West attempts to put a spanner in the works by pre-empting with three diamonds. North passes, expecting his partner to take some action. South elects to bid three no trumps and North raises to four no trumps, which in this sequence is obviously natural, not an inquiry for aces. South probably ought to pass, as he lacks a long suit, but in an excess of zeal he ventures six no trumps. Six clubs would, of course, be a better contract.

Against six no trumps West leads the five of clubs. There are five club tricks on top, three hearts with the aid of the finesse, two spades and one diamond. That is eleven tricks, but unfortunately South cannot rely on the fourth heart, because he has only one entry to the table.

How, then, can declarer arrive at twelve tricks? Study the position after four rounds of clubs and two rounds of hearts:

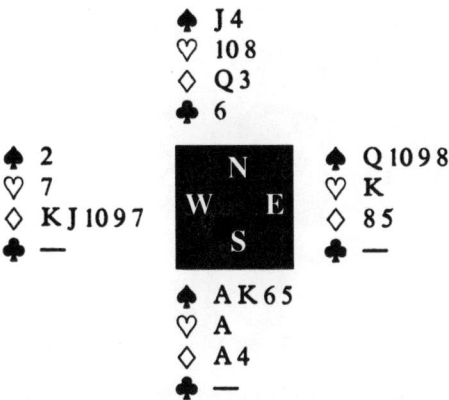

The lead is in dummy. If you haven't seen how South makes his contract, look back to Example 21, then return to this deal.

Correct! On the fifth club South discards the ace of diamonds. He then takes the ace of hearts, ace and king of spades, followed by a low diamond. North's queen of diamonds thus becomes an entry for the ten of hearts.

Example 29

You will have become accustomed by now to the idea of discarding a master card to facilitate the run of a suit. Like North at the table, you will not be impressed by the way South handled his contract of six spades on the following deal:

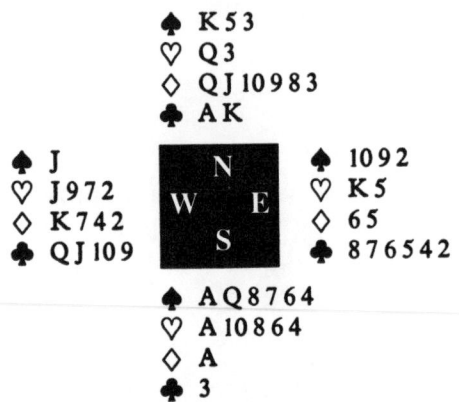

♠ K 5 3
♡ Q 3
♢ Q J 10 9 8 3
♣ A K

♠ J
♡ J 9 7 2
♢ K 7 4 2
♣ Q J 10 9

♠ 10 9 2
♡ K 5
♢ 6 5
♣ 8 7 6 5 4 2

♠ A Q 8 7 6 4
♡ A 10 8 6 4
♢ A
♣ 3

West led the queen of clubs, won by dummy's ace. South came to hand with the ace of diamonds and led a low heart to the queen and king. East returned the ten of spades, which was won in dummy. South played a heart to the ace and attempted to ruff the third round, but East overruffed and played his last trump. South had to lose another heart and finished an inglorious two down.

'I had to find the hearts 3—3,' said South morosely. 'I would have liked to play on the diamonds, but the ace was in the way.'

'Then why not remove it?' suggested North. 'Discard the ace of diamonds on the king of clubs at trick two, then run the queen of diamonds. You lose to the king, but that is all.'

West remarked that if the play went like this he would not part with his king of diamonds. It is, indeed, often good play to retain for as long as possible a control in declarer's main side suit. However, this would not help the defence on the present occasion. If the queen and jack of diamonds are allowed to hold, South plays a third round. East may put in the nine of spades to protect his partner's king of diamonds, but South simply overruffs and plays the ace of spades, followed by the six of spades to dummy's king. The next diamond ruff brings down the king, the four of spades is led to dummy's five, and South's remaining heart losers go away on the last two diamonds. This way, declarer makes an overtrick.

Example 30

The next hand belongs to this series on unblocking plays, though it ends in a more advanced form of play, the squeeze.

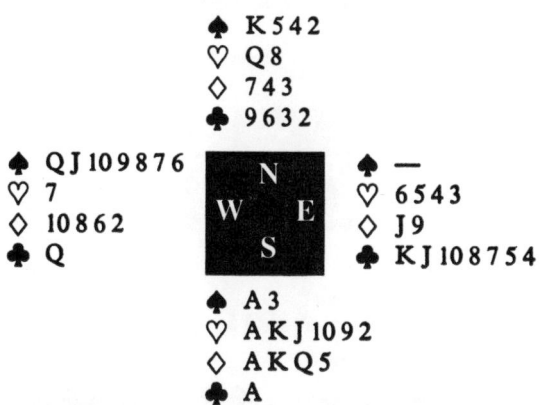

                  ♠ K 5 4 2
                  ♡ Q 8
                  ◇ 7 4 3
                  ♣ 9 6 3 2

    ♠ Q J 10 9 8 7 6   ♠ —
    ♡ 7   ♡ 6 5 4 3
    ◇ 10 8 6 2   ◇ J 9
    ♣ Q   ♣ K J 10 8 7 5 4

                  ♠ A 3
                  ♡ A K J 10 9 2
                  ◇ A K Q 5
                  ♣ A

West deals and opens with a pre-emptive bid of three spades. This is passed round to South, who doubles (for take-out). North bids three no trumps and South propels himself straightaway into six hearts.

West leads the queen of spades, which East ruffs. This is the decisive moment. If South plays low he will need either to find the diamonds 3—3 or to ruff the fourth round safely. As the cards lie, neither chance will succeed, for when the top diamonds are played off, East will ruff. (It would be correct to play off the diamonds before drawing trumps, because of the chance of finding the same defender with short diamonds and short trumps.)

As there is no chance that he will be able to make the ace and king of spades separately, South should unblock the ace of spades at trick one. His position is then much more fluid. After the ace of clubs has won the second trick, the best continuation is a heart to the queen and a club ruff, on which West shows out.

An expert in squeeze play would be able to claim the contract at this point, for if West has the long diamonds he will be squeezed in spades and diamonds, and if East has the long diamonds he will be squeezed in diamonds and clubs.

Preparing for either possibility, South plays off three rounds of trumps, arriving at this position:

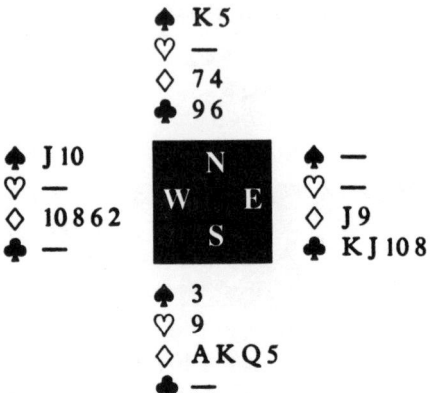

On the nine of hearts West is forced to unguard either spades or diamonds. Note that the North hand has become quite useful, but only because of the unblock of the ace of spades at trick one.

Example 31

Certain combinations must be tackled early on lest a block arises. The spade holding on the deal below is a frequent example.

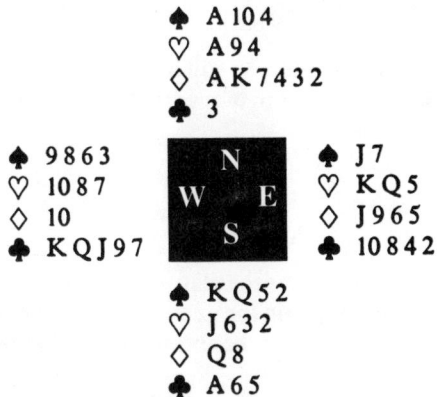

```
              ♠ A 10 4
              ♡ A 9 4
              ◇ A K 7 4 3 2
              ♣ 3
  ♠ 9 8 6 3        N        ♠ J 7
  ♡ 10 8 7    W       E     ♡ K Q 5
  ◇ 10           S          ◇ J 9 6 5
  ♣ K Q J 9 7               ♣ 10 8 4 2
              ♠ K Q 5 2
              ♡ J 6 3 2
              ◇ Q 8
              ♣ A 6 5
```

South is in three no trumps, and when West leads the king of clubs and the dummy goes down, declarer sees that he would have had good chances in six diamonds or six no trumps; all the more reason not to let three no trumps slip away!

It is correct, naturally, to hold off the first two rounds of clubs, because the same opponent might hold three clubs and four diamonds. What should South discard from dummy meanwhile? He can let go two hearts or, slightly better, one heart and one diamond, but must keep the three spades.

Because the main chance appears to lie in the diamond suit, declarer may be tempted to attack this suit when he wins with the ace of clubs. But alas, West shows out on the second round. Declarer might continue diamonds, hoping that East had no more clubs, but probably he would test the spades first, because if spades were 3—3, he would have nine tricks.

When the ace and king of spades are led out, the jack falls, but because of his earlier misplay South cannot take advantage. He can cash the ten of spades but has no entry back to hand to make the queen.

As four tricks in spades would give him game without the aid of a diamond break, it was essential to allow for the possibility of the jack being doubleton. Before releasing the queen of diamonds, South must play off the ace and king of spades; then he can cash the ten and return to the queen of diamonds to make the queen of spades.

There are many other combinations where the possibility of a block must be foreseen:

$$A K Q 4$$
$$8\,7\,5\,3 \qquad J\,10$$
$$9\,6\,2$$

Declarer must broach this suit while he still has a side entry to the table; otherwise he will not be able to take advantage of the drop of the J 10 doubleton.

$$J\,6\,3$$
$$9\,8\,5\,2 \qquad Q\,7$$
$$A\,K\,10\,4$$

Here, again, declarer must not leave the play until too late. He finesses the ten and cashes the ace, dropping the queen. If at this point he has no side entry to his own hand he will not be able to make the king and jack separately.

Example 32

When you are about to play a contract, try to form a complete plan, remembering that one wrong join may cause the downfall of an entire structure.

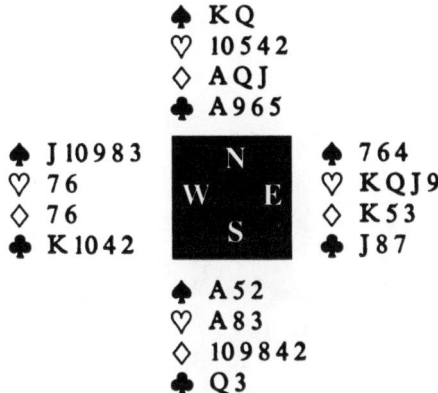

♠ KQ
♡ 10542
◇ AQJ
♣ A965

♠ J10983
♡ 76
◇ 76
♣ K1042

♠ 764
♡ KQJ9
◇ K53
♣ J87

♠ A52
♡ A83
◇ 109842
♣ Q3

South plays in three no trumps and West leads the jack of spades.

It would be poor play, obviously, to cross to the ace of hearts for a diamond finesse, for even if the finesse won, South would be short of entries to derive any benefit. Furthermore, only four diamonds are needed for game, as five tricks are readily available in the other suits.

Having arrived at this conclusion, South wins the first spade in dummy and leads out ace and queen of diamonds. Recognizing that the best way to block the run of the diamonds is to take the king at once, East wins and leads the king of hearts.

South, who was expecting a spade continuation, holds off. East follows with the queen of hearts and South wins, as his best chance now is to find East with the king of clubs and he wants to retain a guard in hearts. He crosses to the jack of diamonds, belatedly cashes the second spade in dummy, and leads a low club to the queen. West wins with the king and the contract is now doomed.

The declarer made a good general plan when he decided to play off ace and queen of diamonds, but he did not foresee the position that would arise if the defenders switched to hearts instead of continuing spades. All he needs to do is cash a second spade early on. Then, after ace and queen of diamonds, followed by a heart from East, he can discard the blocking jack of diamonds on the ace of spades.

Example 33

There is no end to the number of contracts that are lost because the declarer has failed to count his top tricks and ensure that none of them run away. How many players, for example, would set about the following deal in the correct way?

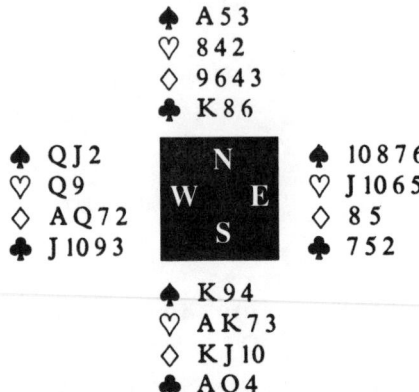

```
              ♠ A 5 3
              ♡ 8 4 2
              ◇ 9 6 4 3
              ♣ K 8 6

♠ Q J 2            N            ♠ 10 8 7 6
♡ Q 9         W        E       ♡ J 10 6 5
◇ A Q 7 2                      ◇ 8 5
♣ J 10 9 3         S          ♣ 7 5 2

              ♠ K 9 4
              ♡ A K 7 3
              ◇ K J 10
              ♣ A Q 4
```

South is in three no trumps and West leads the jack of clubs. Declarer wins in dummy and finesses the jack of diamonds, losing to the queen.

If West inertly continues clubs, declarer will easily make his contract, but a good player in West's position will note that South is attempting to develop a long diamond and will attack dummy's entry by leading the queen of spades. Declarer wins with the king and tries to slip through the ten of diamonds, but West goes up with the ace and continues with the jack of spades. After dummy's ace of spades has been forced out, South can play a diamond to the king but cannot return to dummy to make the nine. He tries to develop a trick in hearts, but the 4—2 break defeats him and he is left with only eight tricks.

How easy this contract is, if declarer notes at the beginning that he has three tricks in clubs, two hearts, two in spades, and a minimum of two in diamonds! To make sure of the diamond tricks, he must win the club lead with the ace and launch diamonds from his own hand. The king is slightly better than the jack, because it may bring down a singleton queen. West may hold off the first diamond, but South continues with the jack and cannot be prevented from establishing a further trick with the nine.

Example 34

When ruffs are needed in a suit contract it is sometimes impossible to avoid being landed in the wrong hand, with no convenient entry to enable the trumps to be drawn. The solution may lie in a ducking play which appears to give up the chance of a trick.

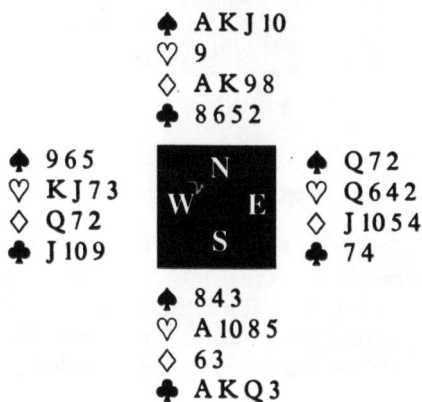

```
              ♠ A K J 10
              ♡ 9
              ◊ A K 9 8
              ♣ 8 6 5 2
  ♠ 9 6 5                    ♠ Q 7 2
  ♡ K J 7 3     N           ♡ Q 6 4 2
  ◊ Q 7 2    W     E        ◊ J 10 5 4
  ♣ J 10 9      S            ♣ 7 4
              ♠ 8 4 3
              ♡ A 10 8 5
              ◊ 6 3
              ♣ A K Q 3
```

South is in six clubs and West's lead of the jack of clubs creates an entry problem.

Declarer must assume that clubs are 3—2. If he can make four tricks in spades, one heart ruff will be sufficient, but if there is a spade loser, he will need two ruffs in hearts. Let us try some sequences of play that seem plausible.

First, South may put the spade finesse to the test at trick two. The best defence is for East to win and lead a second trump. Now South, needing two heart ruffs, may play the ace of hearts and ruff a heart, return to hand with a diamond ruff, and trump another heart; but now he is on the table, with no way of getting back to hand to draw the outstanding trump.

Anticipating this situation, South may take a heart ruff at once, return to the king of clubs, and ruff a second heart. Then he can return with a diamond ruff and draw the last trump, but when the jack of spades is finessed, East will win and meanly cash the fourth round of hearts.

It is right to begin with a heart ruff, but let us look at the position after the ruff has been taken:

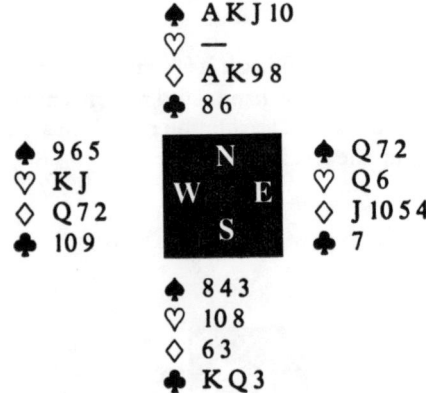

At this point the best play is the jack of spades from dummy! The defenders win and cannot do better than lead a second trump. Now South ruffs another heart with dummy's last trump, returns to hand with a ruff of the third diamond, and draws the outstanding trump. His remaining heart loser goes away safely on the fourth round of spades.

This deal is quite a tricky exercise in communication play. The critical move is the surrender of a spade trick at a moment when dummy can take care of any lead by the defence.

Example 35

When planning the play of a hand where there will surely be communication problems, it is essential to take into account that opponents will make your task more difficult by holding up their master cards.

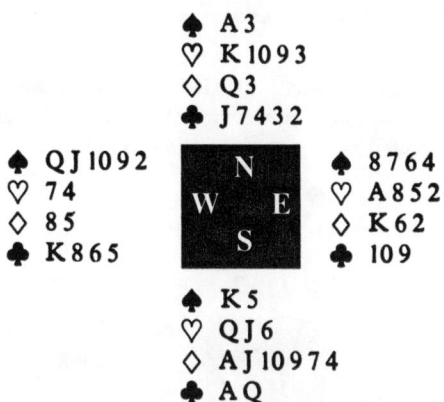

South plays in six diamonds and West leads the queen of spades.

Declarer must assume, first, that the diamond finesse is right, because he is certainly going to lose one trick in hearts. But the diamond finesse alone will not be enough: there is still a possible loser in clubs.

Perhaps the long heart in dummy will provide a discard for the queen of clubs. With this in mind, South wins the spade lead in dummy, finesses the queen of diamonds successfully, and picks up the trumps. Then he plays the queen of hearts, followed by the jack of hearts, which he overtakes with the king. East again holds off, and now the only hope is the club finesse, which fails.

What has gone wrong? It is quite a difficult hand, but the answer is that South has not taken advantage of the possibility of communication within the heart suit itself. The best play is to win the spade lead in hand with the king and lead the jack of hearts, overtaking with the king. Say that East wins and leads a club: South goes up with the ace, enters dummy with the ace of spades for the diamond finesse, and later discards the queen of clubs on a long heart. And if East refuses to win the first heart? Then South takes the diamond finesse and later clears the hearts, with the ace of spades still on the table as an entry card.

Example 36

As any player knows from experience, a 3—2 break of five outstanding cards is a good deal more likely than a 4—1 break. The figures given by the mathematicians are 68% for 3—2, 28% for 4—1. It is still necessary to take as many precautions as possible against a 4—1 break; 28% is not an amount to be spurned.

The play of the following hand was a little ironical: South was aware of the danger of a 4—1 break, took a precaution that was not strictly necessary, and then spoiled his chance by failing to unblock.

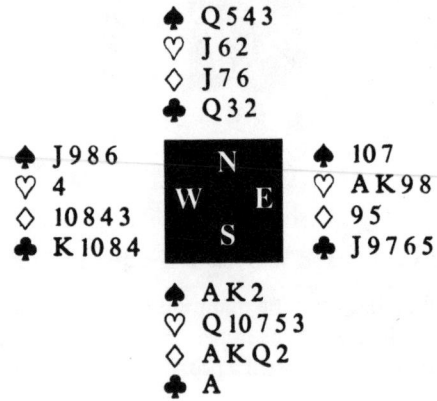

```
              ♠ Q 5 4 3
              ♡ J 6 2
              ◇ J 7 6
              ♣ Q 3 2
  ♠ J 9 8 6                  ♠ 10 7
  ♡ 4            N           ♡ A K 9 8
  ◇ 10 8 4 3   W   E         ◇ 9 5
  ♣ K 10 8 4      S          ♣ J 9 7 6 5
              ♠ A K 2
              ♡ Q 10 7 5 3
              ◇ A K Q 2
              ♣ A
```

South was in four hearts and West's lead of the four of clubs ran to the singleton ace. A low heart went to the jack and king, and East played back a club.

The club return, in preference, say, to a diamond up to the weakness, was an indication that East had long trumps and wanted to force the declarer to ruff. Reflecting that he could afford to lose two trumps and a club, South discarded a low diamond, allowing West's king to win. Now West led a spade; South won in dummy and played a heart to the ten, but he had no entry back to the table and had to lose two more tricks to East's K 9 of hearts.

If South was not going to ruff the club return at trick three, it was essential to unblock in spades or diamonds, retaining two entries to the table; then East's hearts can be picked up for the loss of only one more trick.

Analysing the hand later, South came to the conclusion that his 'safety' play of declining to ruff the club was an illusion. He can ruff, enter dummy with a spade, and lead the next heart from dummy. East's best defence is to go up with the ace and lead another club. South passes this and makes the rest of the tricks quite easily. (If East ducks the second heart, South wins and plays on the other suits, allowing East to make two more trump tricks, but nothing else.)

Example 37

Blocking plays, in general, are more difficult than unblocking plays. We gave some examples earlier on of blocking plays by the declarer. The deal below illustrates a position where a defender may have a chance for a blocking play that is well known but is usually missed at the table.

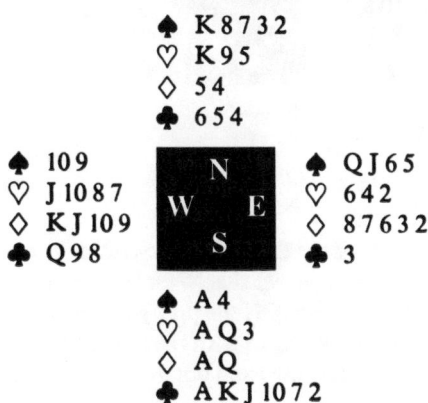

```
              ♠ K 8 7 3 2
              ♡ K 9 5
              ◇ 5 4
              ♣ 6 5 4
   ♠ 10 9                    ♠ Q J 6 5
   ♡ J 10 8 7                ♡ 6 4 2
   ◇ K J 10 9                ◇ 8 7 6 3 2
   ♣ Q 9 8                   ♣ 3
              ♠ A 4
              ♡ A Q 3
              ◇ A Q
              ♣ A K J 10 7 2
```

South is in six clubs and West leads the jack of hearts, which runs to the declarer's ace. With nine cards, missing the queen, it is normal to play for the drop, unless there are special indications, so declarer plays off the ace and king of clubs, discovering the 3—1 break when East discards a low diamond.

The problem now is to avoid the risk of the diamond finesse. There are chances to get a long spade going, so South plays the ace of spades, a spade to the king, and a third spade, which he ruffs with the jack of clubs.

Now West has his first opportunity for a good play. If he overruffs, he leaves declarer with two entries to dummy—the king of hearts and the six of clubs; this will enable South to establish a long spade for a diamond discard.

West discards a diamond, therefore. The position is now:

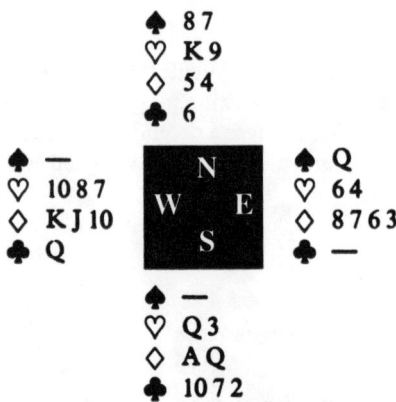

At this point South may lead the three of hearts, intending, if West plays low, to finesse the nine. (Remember that West led the jack of hearts, presumably from J 10 and others.) If the play goes like this, West can thwart the declarer's plan by going in with the ten of hearts. This fine blocking play prevents the dummy from obtaining two entries to set up a spade winner.

Declarer can do better, however, in the diagram position. He should exit at once with a trump. Now, if West leads the ten of hearts, dummy wins and South unblocks the queen; then a spade ruff, a heart to the nine, and the queen of diamonds goes away on the fifth spade.

Example 38

Life is short, time passes quickly, and how often do you wish that you could do two things at the same time! When the opportunity arises to do just that, be sure to take it.

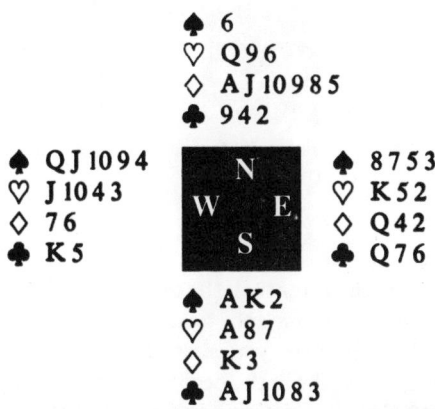

```
              ♠ 6
              ♡ Q96
              ◇ AJ10985
              ♣ 942
♠ QJ1094              ♠ 8753
♡ J1043      N        ♡ K52
◇ 76      W     E.    ◇ Q42
♣ K5         S        ♣ Q76
              ♠ AK2
              ♡ A87
              ◇ K3
              ♣ AJ1083
```

You are in three no trumps and West leads the queen of spades. Make your plan without looking at the opposing hands and before reading on.

If your only chance were to make six diamond tricks, it would be correct to finesse the jack on the second round, but this is not attractive here for two reasons: one is that, if the finesse lost, you would make only one trick in diamonds and the defenders would establish their spade suit before you had begun to play on clubs; the other is that four tricks in clubs would be enough for game, assuming you made at least ace and king of diamonds. Meanwhile, there is a chance that you may drop a doubleton queen.

Let's look at three possible plans and decide which is best.

1) You win with the king of spades and lead the jack of clubs from hand. You are planning, in effect, to find West with a doubleton or singleton honour. Best defence for West is to let the jack run to the queen. Later, after playing ace and king of diamonds, you will have to take the right view of the clubs and drop the king.

2) You may begin with the king and another diamond to the ace. The queen does not fall, so you now play a club to the ten and king. You hope later to drop the queen, but this plan fails as the cards lie.

3) Now let's try another way of tackling the diamonds. You lead low and put in the jack. If East wins, the hand is over, for on the next round you will of course overtake the king of diamonds with the ace. If East is smart enough to duck, you switch to the two of clubs, losing the trick to West. You take the next spade, lead the king of diamonds and overtake. The queen does not fall, but now you lead the nine of clubs and pick up the tricks you need in this suit.

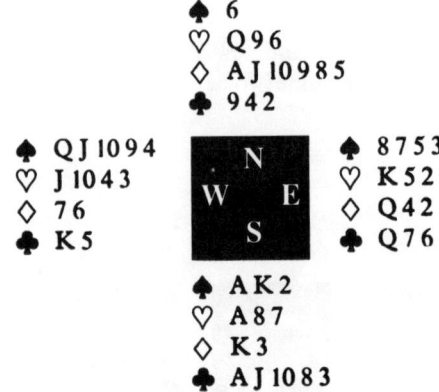

♠ 6
♡ Q96
◇ AJ10985
♣ 942

♠ QJ1094
♡ J1043
◇ 76
♣ K5

♠ 8753
♡ K52
◇ Q42
♣ Q76

♠ AK2
♡ A87
◇ K3
♣ AJ1083

You see how plan (3) is much better than the others? By leading a low diamond to the jack, you give yourself the best chance to bring in the diamond suit, and, at the same time, you create a second entry to dummy which allows you to play the clubs in the best possible way, losing two tricks only when West holds both the king and queen of clubs.

One small additional point: it would not be good play, when attacking clubs from dummy, to lead the nine on the first round. If this lost to a singleton honour, you would not be able later to pick up K x x x or Q x x x in the East hand.

Example 39

The next hand shows something a little different: how to take advantage of a blocked position in defence.

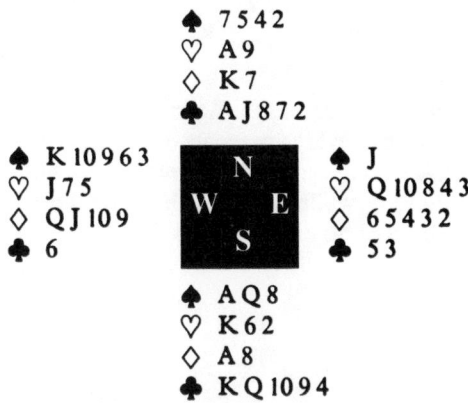

```
              ♠ 7542
              ♡ A9
              ◇ K7
              ♣ AJ872
♠ K10963                    ♠ J
♡ J75          N            ♡ Q10843
◇ QJ109      W   E          ◇ 65432
♣ 6            S            ♣ 53
              ♠ AQ8
              ♡ K62
              ◇ A8
              ♣ KQ1094
```

South is in six clubs and West leads the queen of diamonds.

Even if the declarer has not made a study of elimination play, he will probably play the cards in the right order. After drawing trumps he cashes the second diamond and plays three rounds of hearts, finishing with a ruff on the table. The position is now:

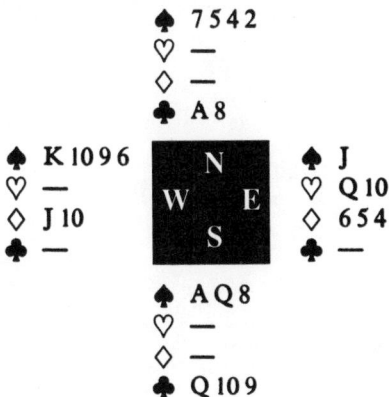

```
              ♠ 7542
              ♡ —
              ◇ —
              ♣ A8
♠ K1096                     ♠ J
♡ —            N            ♡ Q10
◇ J10        W   E          ◇ 654
♣ —            S            ♣ —
              ♠ AQ8
              ♡ —
              ◇ —
              ♣ Q109
```

South leads a spade from dummy. If East plays any low card, South can ensure the contract by putting in the eight, leaving West on play. As the cards lie on this occasion, East plays the jack. Now South can do better than finesse: he plays low, and, as East has no more spades, the defence is helpless. The play would be the same, of course, if East's card were the nine or ten.

Looking at this position from the angle of the defenders, we find that singleton honours tend to be a liability. Suppose that a side suit lies like this towards the end of the play:

$$x\,x\,x$$
$$A\,J\,x \qquad K$$
$$Q\,x$$

Apart from the suit shown, declarer has only trumps in his own hand and dummy. Now East's singleton king prevents the defence from taking two tricks, as, if East is left on lead, he will have to lead a suit which declarer can ruff in dummy, while discarding his second spade. If possible, therefore, East must discard his king earlier in the play.

Example 40

It happens occasionally that declarer needs to unblock one of his own
high cards in a suit that he proposes to establish.

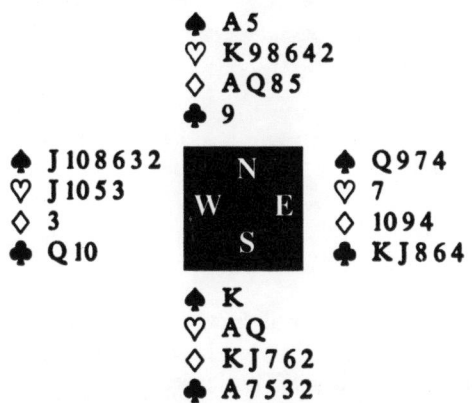

```
                    ♠ A 5
                    ♡ K 9 8 6 4 2
                    ◇ A Q 8 5
                    ♣ 9
    ♠ J 10 8 6 3 2          N          ♠ Q 9 7 4
    ♡ J 10 5 3        W           E    ♡ 7
    ◇ 3                     S          ◇ 10 9 4
    ♣ Q 10                             ♣ K J 8 6 4
                    ♠ K
                    ♡ A Q
                    ◇ K J 7 6 2
                    ♣ A 7 5 3 2
```

South is in seven diamonds and West leads the jack of spades. Declarer
wins and draws two rounds of trumps, West discarding a spade.

The hearts look a better proposition than the clubs, so declarer's next
move may be to draw the third trump and cash the ace and queen of
hearts. Now the 4—1 break defeats him, for his only entry to dummy is a
trump. The best he can do is cash the ace of clubs, ruff a club, and take
two discards on the ace of spades and king of hearts; that leaves him still
with a losing club.

It would be better play, after cashing the ace and king of diamonds, to lay
down the ace and queen of hearts before drawing the third trump. This
would gain if, by chance, the same hand held four hearts and the
outstanding trump. As the cards lie, however, East ruffs the second heart.

It was a mistake to draw two trumps immediately. After one high trump
from hand, South should cash the ace of hearts and then play a second
diamond to the ace. Observe the difference:

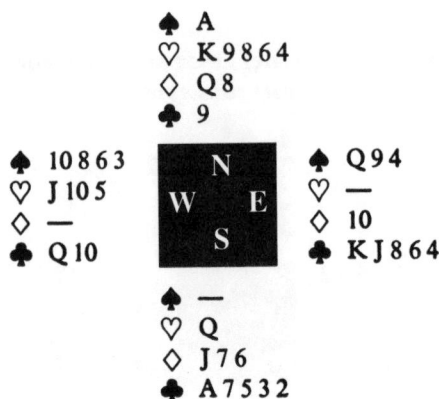

```
                    ♠ A
                    ♡ K 9 8 6 4
                    ◇ Q 8
                    ♣ 9
    ♠ 10 8 6 3          N          ♠ Q 9 4
    ♡ J 10 5                       ♡ —
    ◇ —         W          E       ◇ 10
    ♣ Q 10          S              ♣ K J 8 6 4
                    ♠ —
                    ♡ Q
                    ◇ J 7 6
                    ♣ A 7 5 3 2
```

Now South makes the critical play of discarding the queen of hearts on the ace of spades. Then he ruffs a low heart, crosses to the queen of diamonds, and ruffs another heart. This leaves the dummy high, with a trump as an entry for the hearts.

It may seem strange that the only way to get the hearts going is to discard one of the high honours, but if you play the hand over in several ways, you will find that this is so.

Example 41

Very often a declarer will want to develop a suit without letting a particular opponent into the lead. Straightforward play may allow the opponents a chance to unblock so that, from their point of view, the right defender will win the critical trick. The declarer may be able to avoid this by playing his cards in the correct order.

On the deal below, South aims to establish his ninth trick in clubs, but after the first trick he knows he dare not let East into the lead.

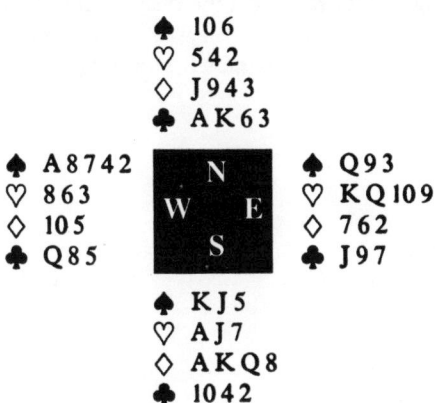

```
                    ♠ 10 6
                    ♡ 5 4 2
                    ◇ J 9 4 3
                    ♣ A K 6 3
     ♠ A 8 7 4 2         N         ♠ Q 9 3
     ♡ 8 6 3        W         E    ♡ K Q 10 9
     ◇ 10 5             S         ◇ 7 6 2
     ♣ Q 8 5                      ♣ J 9 7
                    ♠ K J 5
                    ♡ A J 7
                    ◇ A K Q 8
                    ♣ 10 4 2
```

South is in three no trumps and West leads the four of spades. Declarer plays low from dummy (it cannot gain to put in the ten) and East puts in the nine. Note that this is good play by East: if South has A J x, he will have a double stop anyway, but if he has K J x, he can be held to one trick by this finesse of the nine.

South wins with the jack and can see only eight top tricks. The hearts offer no hope, because even if East has the K Q under the A J, he will split his honours on the first round and gain the lead to play a spade through the king. The only chance for a ninth trick lies in clubs; they may be 3—3 or there may even be a doubleton Q J.

While developing the clubs, South must try to prevent East from gaining the lead. He begins with a low club to the ace. If he follows with the king of clubs from dummy, he makes it quite easy for West to unblock the queen of clubs. Instead, South must return to hand with a diamond and then lead the second club. If West plays the queen now, he will be allowed to hold the trick, and if he plays low, he will be forced to win the third round.

Perhaps you think it would do no harm for South to play a couple of high diamonds before leading a club? But against an expert defender this might be fatal. South must return to hand with a third diamond to play the next club, and at this point West will have a chance to dispose of his queen of clubs.

The declarer's manoeuvre on this deal goes by the unprepossessing name of 'avoidance play'. It has innumerable variations. This is one that is usually misplayed:

$$\begin{array}{c c}
& \text{Q 10 7 4 2} \\
\text{K 5} & \text{J 9 3} \\
& \text{A 8 6}
\end{array}$$

South wants to get this suit going without letting East into the lead. If he begins with the ace, then any respectable player in West's position will unblock the king and East will win the third round. Instead, declarer should begin with a low card. If West plays low, South goes up with the queen and lets West win the next round with the king.

Example 42

We conclude with an example of a form of play that is very simple in some of its manifestations but can easily be missed when the setting is more complex. Nobody who had played bridge for more than a week would go wrong with this combination:

```
        A 9 7 4 2
Q 5              J 10 6
        K 8 3
```

Playing in no trumps, South wants to make four tricks in this suit and has no sure side entry to the table. He would, of course, play the king and then duck the next round, to be sure of communication when the suit was breaking 3—2.

The same principle arises on the deal below, but how many very experienced players would miss the correct play.

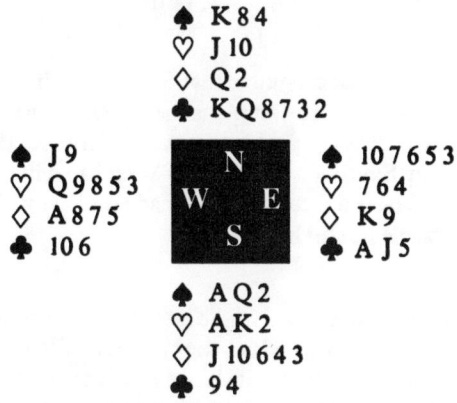

```
                ♠ K 8 4
                ♡ J 10
                ◇ Q 2
                ♣ K Q 8 7 3 2
♠ J 9                           ♠ 10 7 6 5 3
♡ Q 9 8 5 3        N            ♡ 7 6 4
◇ A 8 7 5      W       E        ◇ K 9
♣ 10 6            S             ♣ A J 5
                ♠ A Q 2
                ♡ A K 2
                ◇ J 10 6 4 3
                ♣ 9 4
```

South is in three no trumps, West leads the five of hearts, and dummy's jack holds the first trick.

Declarer will obviously want to play on clubs, and it is tempting to cross to hand with the queen of spades and lead a club to the queen. This would work well enough if West held A x or A x x, or if East held the ace and took the trick. However, East need not be a genius, with A J x, to let the queen hold. (It would be good play, also, to duck with A x.) South comes back to the ace of spades to lead another club. East wins and now the club suit is effectively shut out, because there is only one entry to the table.

South can afford to lose two club tricks but not to lose touch with the dummy. A low club from the table is as good as anything at trick two. East wins and leads a heart, but South is comfortably in control. After taking the heart he leads his second club towards the K Q and has the king of spades as an entry when he wants it.

There are some very tricky positions around this theme, both in attack and defence.

<pre>
        A Q J 5 3
  7 4   K 10 8 2
        9 6
</pre>

South needs specifically three tricks from this suit and has one side entry to the dummy. If he begins with a low card to the queen, East can block the run of the suit by holding up his king. South does better to play low on the first round, letting East win with the ten. Then (assuming that dummy's entry cannot be driven out immediately) declarer will be able to establish the three tricks he needs.

The commonest occasion for this type of play in defence occurs when the suit led is like this:

<pre>
        8 5 2
  7 3   K Q 10 9 4
        A J 6
</pre>

West leads the seven and East can judge that South, who has bid no trumps over him, holds A J x. If East plays the queen, South will duck and East will need two entries to get his suit going. Instead, East should put in the nine, forcing South to win. Now, if West can win the first defensive trick, he will have a second card to lead and East will be able to establish his suit while he still has his entry.

Some of the plays we have described in the later examples have been quite advanced, it is true. Nevertheless, they are not difficult once the general principle of blocking and unblocking are understood. They involve no deep analysis, just familiarity with the type of play that is needed. Don't be disturbed if on occasions you make an unblocking play, or a hold-up play, that turns out to have been misconceived. If you are alive to the possibilities, you will save many more contracts than you give away.

Safety Plays

Safety plays are a form of insurance against a bad break.

Suppose, for example, that a normal division of the adverse cards would enable you to lose no tricks at all in the suit that interests you, whereas against very bad distribution you might lose two tricks; if there is a way to lose just one trick, *whatever the distribution*, then a safety play is available and you must employ it whenever the contract depends on losing not more than one trick. Putting it another way, you sacrifice a trick when the distribution is favourable, but when it is unfavourable you make sure you do not lose two tricks.

It is essential to know all the standard safety plays; they will reward you many times over. The occasional overtricks you give up, worth 20 or 30 points apiece, will be amply compensated by the thousands of points you will gain by ensuring your contract.

A special point about safety plays is that it is not necessary to count the hands or to know the adverse distribution: all you need is to realize that a particular suit may break badly. It is enough, when you are playing a contract that seems to be lay-down, to pause and say to yourself: 'Can I lose this contract if the breaks are extremely bad?' If the answer is yes, then look for a safety play that will protect you against such distribution.

In this account of safety plays we have not aimed to present difficult or spectacular coups, but problems of a type you will meet often and will readily recognize. Note that to execute these plays it is not necessary to reconstruct or count the adverse hands, as is required for most forms of end-play.

When you have read and re-read the example hands, you will have learned to foresee the danger of bad distribution. You may meet slightly different problems at the table, but you will have mastered certain principles and will be able to apply them to a variety of new situations.

Example 1

You hold between dummy and yourself eight cards of a suit including
the ace, king and ten. These cards may all be in the same hand or in
opposite hands. Your object is to lose not more than one trick in the suit.
First lead the ace and then lead a low card, intending to put in the ten if
the left-hand opponent has also played low. These are typical holdings:

K 10 x x x	K 10 x x	A K 10 x
A x x	A x x x	x x x x
A K 10 x x	K 10 8 x x x	A K 10 9 x x
x x x	A 9	x x

If the finesse of the ten loses to the jack or queen, then the distribution
must be 3—2 and the remaining honour will fall under the king on the
next round. Meanwhile, you insure against Q J x x on the left. If these
cards are on the right, nothing can be done. Note that in the last two
examples, where declarer has only a doubleton, it is necessary to add some
strengthening cards; otherwise a defender with, say, Q J 9 x could render
the safety play ineffective by splitting his honours on the second round.

You play the following hand as South in a contract of four hearts:

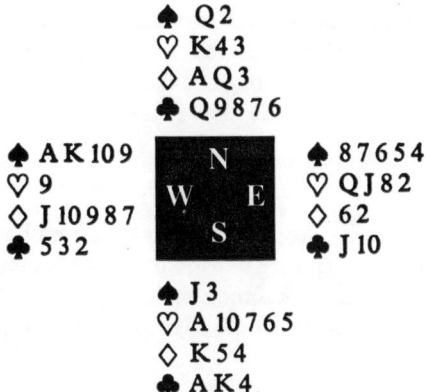

```
              ♠ Q 2
              ♡ K 4 3
              ◇ A Q 3
              ♣ Q 9 8 7 6

♠ A K 10 9        N        ♠ 8 7 6 5 4
♡ 9          W        E    ♡ Q J 8 2
◇ J 10 9 8 7      S        ◇ 6 2
♣ 5 3 2                    ♣ J 10

              ♠ J 3
              ♡ A 10 7 6 5
              ◇ K 5 4
              ♣ A K 4
```

West leads the king and ace of spades, then switches to the jack of diamonds. South wins and sees that there are no more losers outside the trump suit; he must, therefore, avoid losing two trump tricks.

South leads the king of hearts from dummy, East plays the two and West the nine. On the next heart East plays the eight and now South must put in the ten. If East began with Q J 8 2, South will win this trick and lose only one heart. If East began with Q 8 2, West will capture the ten with the jack, but East's queen will fall under the ace on the next round.

Note that it would not help East, as the cards lie, to play the queen or jack on the second round. South would win, cross to dummy with a diamond or a club, and then lead up to the 10 7 6, again losing one trick. East does better not to split his honours in this type of situation; then he will make two tricks if South neglects to make the safety play.

Example 2

You hold between dummy and yourself nine cards of a suit including the ace and queen, with or without the ten, the ace and queen being in the same hand. Your object is to lose not more than one trick in the suit. You should lay down the ace, then lead up to the queen.

$$A\,Q\,10\,x\,x \qquad x\,x\,x$$
$$x\,x\,x\,x \qquad A\,Q\,x\,x\,x\,x$$

In the first example if the ace drops a singleton king from East, you lose no trick at all, as you can return to hand to finesse the ten. In the second example you lose one trick if the king is single on your left, but if you had finessed the queen you would have lost a second trick to East's J 10 x.

You play the following hand as South in a contract of six spades:

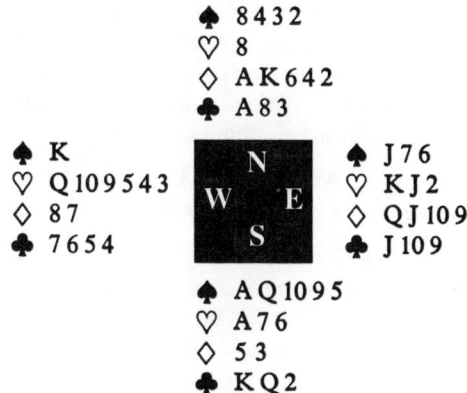

♠ 8432
♡ 8
◇ AK642
♣ A83

♠ K
♡ Q109543
◇ 87
♣ 7654

♠ J76
♡ KJ2
◇ QJ109
♣ J109

♠ AQ1095
♡ A76
◇ 53
♣ KQ2

West leads the eight of diamonds and you win with the king in dummy.
You see that there are no losers outside the trump suit; therefore your sole
concern is to avoid losing two tricks in spades.

If you lead a spade from dummy and finesse the queen, losing to West's
king, you will have to guess on the next round whether to play for the drop
(by leading the ace) or to take a finesse against the jack. You would be
in the same dilemma if you finessed the ten on the first round and lost to
the jack: West might hold the K J or the jack might be single.

The correct play is to lay down the ace on the first round. If West
follows with a low card, you re-enter dummy and lead towards the queen.
If West sits over you with the K J x, there is nothing to be done, but if
East has three cards, or if the distribution is 2—2, you lose just one trick.

When the king is single, as in the diagram above, you lose no tricks at
all, as you can safely cross to dummy and finesse against East's J x.
If West has K J alone, or the jack alone, you lose just one trick. But if you
finesse the queen on the first round, losing to the king, you will have to
'take a view' on the next round, and it is even money that you will do the
wrong thing.

Example 3

You hold with the dummy eight cards of a suit including the ace and queen, these two cards in the same hand. Your object is to lose *not more than two* tricks in the suit. Again, the first play should be to lay down the ace. The situation is analogous to that of the previous example, but it occurs more often. These are common holdings:

$$\begin{array}{ccc} \text{A Q x x} & \text{A Q x x x} & \text{A Q x x x x} \\ \text{x x x x} & \text{x x x} & \text{x x} \end{array}$$

If your play of the ace drops a singleton king, you lose only two tricks in the suit instead of three, as would happen if you took the finesse. If the king does not appear you lead low towards the queen on the next round. Note that if West holds, say, K J x, you lose nothing by refusing the finesse on the first round. Even if West holds K J 10 x, you still lose only two tricks. The difference arises when East holds a singleton king.

When South played the following hand in three no trumps, he had to take certain other factors into consideration.

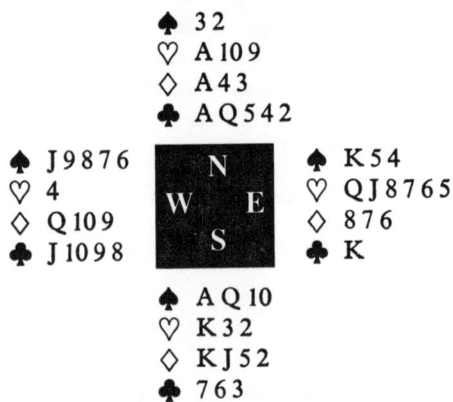

```
                ♠ 3 2
                ♡ A 10 9
                ◇ A 4 3
                ♣ A Q 5 4 2
♠ J 9 8 7 6                    ♠ K 5 4
♡ 4          N                ♡ Q J 8 7 6 5
◇ Q 10 9   W   E              ◇ 8 7 6
♣ J 10 9 8     S              ♣ K
                ♠ A Q 10
                ♡ K 3 2
                ◇ K J 5 2
                ♣ 7 6 3
```

West led the seven of spades (fourth best). East played the king and South won with the ace. (With A Q x South would have held up on the first trick, but the ten makes a big difference, as will shortly appear.) Declarer could count six certain tricks outside the clubs, so three tricks in clubs would be enough. This was clearly a moment for safety play, the more so as it would be extremely inconvenient to allow East to win and play a spade through the Q 10.

South led a club to the ace, therefore, dropping the singleton king. Very lucky, you may think. But there was more to the play than just the chance of catching the king. When South led the club from hand he had these possibilities in mind:

1) If West played the king, he would be allowed to hold the trick and would not be able to attack spades except by leading up to the Q 10.
2) If West played low, and East also played low on the ace, declarer intended to return a club from dummy. West might have J x, and when in with the jack he would be unable to do any damage.
3) Better still, East might hold K x; in that case the clubs would be established for the loss of one trick.
4) Finally, West might hold K J 10 9, but even then he could be held to two tricks in clubs.

After the ace of clubs had dropped the king, South returned a club from dummy. West took his only chance now by leading the jack of spades. He hoped that either South held A Q x, in which case his partner would unblock by playing the ten under the jack, or that South held A Q x x, in which case East's ten would fall, and the queen could be forced out. But West was out of luck. South captured the jack of spades with the queen, gave up a club to establish the suit, and ended up with ten tricks— three spades, three clubs, and four top cards in the red suits.

There is one further point worth noting about the type of safety plays we have been discussing in this section. The same effect may be obtained by *ducking* the first round of the suit instead of playing the ace. If the king is single, it will beat the air—which is better than letting it capture the queen. On many hands it is safer to duck the first round than to play the ace. Suppose the trump suit is distributed in this way:

$$\begin{array}{ccc} & \text{x x x} & \\ \text{K J 10 x} & & \text{x} \\ & \text{A Q x x x} & \end{array}$$

To lay down the ace and later lead up to the queen gives up all control. The declarer will probably be better placed if he ducks the first round and goes up with the ace when East shows out on the second round.

Example 4

You hold with the dummy nine cards of a suit, including the ace, king and queen, but not the ten or jack. Your object is to lose no trick in the suit.

A x x	K 8 x x	K Q 8 x x
K Q 9 x x x	A Q 9 x x	A 9 x x

In each case it is correct to begin with the high card that is on its own—the ace in the first example.

One of the present authors had a bitter experience when the following hand occurred at rubber bridge:

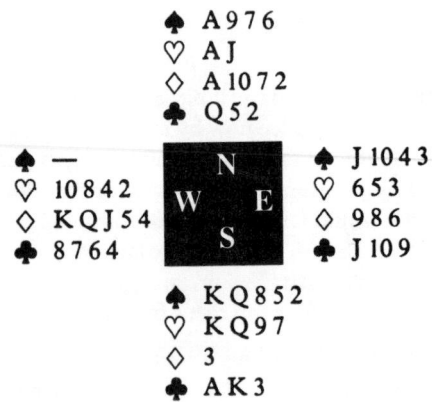

North, the dealer, had agreed to play a strong no trump of 16—18 points, but facing an inexperienced partner he decided to open one no trump rather than one spade. He was a point short for the bid, but hoped to play the hand. Alas! South forced with three spades, followed with a Blackwood four no trumps on the next round, and then propelled himself into seven spades!

West led the king of diamonds, and after putting down his dummy North glimpsed the J 10 4 3 of spades in the East hand. To his horror, he saw his partner begin with a low spade to the king. From that moment it was all over.

South was quite a talented player, but he had not learned his safety plays. The only danger was a 4—0 break in trumps. If West held the four trumps, there would be no way to pick them up without loss. But if East held them, the play of the ace from dummy would disclose the void and there would be no problem then in picking up the J 10 x. On the next round East would play the ten and South the king; then declarer would cross to dummy and finesse against East's J 4.

North was left with the ironical reflection that if he had opened one spade instead of one no trump he would have played the slam contract himself!

Example 5

You hold in dummy and your own hand ten cards of a suit, missing the king and ten. The queen and jack are in different hands and your object is to lose no trick.

J x x x x x	J x x x	Q 9 8 x x
A Q 9 x	A Q 9 x x x	A J x x x

You should lead first the single honour—the jack in the first two examples, the queen in the third.

Suppose that the player who bid the last hand with such fire were to play the following hand in seven hearts:

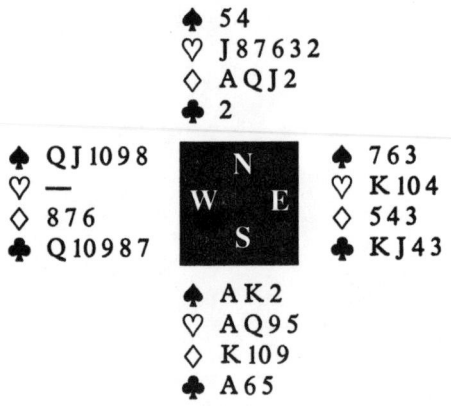

                    ♠ 5 4
                    ♡ J 8 7 6 3 2
                    ◇ A Q J 2
                    ♣ 2

    ♠ Q J 10 9 8   ♠ 7 6 3
    ♡ —   ♡ K 10 4
    ◇ 8 7 6   ◇ 5 4 3
    ♣ Q 10 9 8 7   ♣ K J 4 3

                    ♠ A K 2
                    ♡ A Q 9 5
                    ◇ K 10 9
                    ♣ A 6 5

West leads the queen of spades and South wins with the ace.
He has three possible ways of entering dummy for a heart finesse: he can ruff the third round of spades, cross to the queen of diamonds, or ruff the second round of clubs. The club ruff, if there has been no adverse bidding, is the safest of these, so South cashes the ace of clubs, ruffs a club, and leads a low heart from the table. East plays the four and South, after deep reflection, the queen.

Now he must lose a trick to the king of hearts. One can imagine
the post-mortem.

South: 'Sorry, partner. I suppose I overbid, but we might have been
luckier.'

Seeing that North is shaking his head, South goes on:

'I took the best chance, didn't I ? I mean, it wouldn't be right to put
in the nine, would it ? Or to play for the drop of a singleton king ?'

North: 'No, you can't play for the drop with ten cards—that would be
well against the odds. But if you are going to finesse, you must lead the
jack from dummy on the first round. If East holds K x, it makes no
difference whether you lead the jack or a small card. But when East has
K 10 x, as on this occasion, leading the jack solves all your problems.
If East plays low, you let the jack run, of course. If he covers, then
West's void is shown up and all you have to do is enter dummy again for a
finesse against the 10 x. Not very difficult!'

Example 6

You and dummy hold nine cards of a suit, missing K 10 9 x. The queen and jack are in separate hands and your object is to lose not more than one trick.

Jxxx   J 8 7 x x   Q x x

A Q 8 x x   A Q x x   A J 8 x x x

As in the previous set of examples, you must begin with the single honour—the jack in the first two examples, the queen in the third.

Suppose you play the following hand in a contract of six clubs:

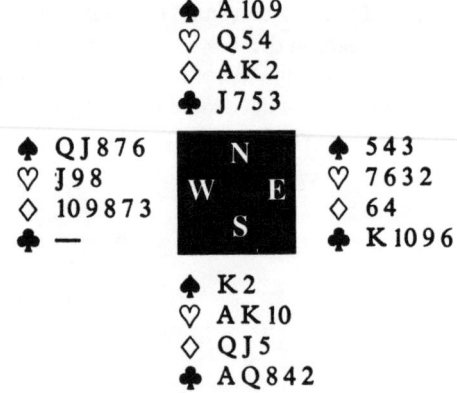

West leads the queen of spades and you win with the ace in dummy. There are no losers outside the trump suit, so all that concerns you is not to lose two club tricks.

If the clubs are 3—1 or 2—2, you will never lose more than one trick. (It is true that you might finesse and then sustain an unlucky ruff. If you held the nine or ten of clubs in addition, you would play the ace first for that reason, but in the present case you have to consider the more likely possibility of a defender holding K 10 9 x.) Suppose, then, that all four clubs are in one hand. If West holds them, you cannot avoid losing two tricks. You concentrate, therefore, on the possibility of East holding K 10 9 x.

Employing the same technique as in the previous examples, you lead the *jack* from dummy. East will probably cover with the king. You win with the ace and return a low club to the seven. East can win this trick but his last two clubs will be exposed to a finesse.

The same style of play is followed when you are missing A 10 9 x, as in these situations:

Q7543   KQ652
KJ82   J873

In the first example you lead the queen from dummy, so that you will be able to pick up A 10 9 x in the East hand. In the second example you lead the jack from hand, so that you can pick up West's A 10 9 x. You can achieve the same effect, it is true, by leading a low card away from the hand containing the two honours. The mistake would be to play one of the double honours on the first round, because then you would lose two tricks whenever the suit was divided 4—0.

Example 7

We move now to a different type of safety play, where the way to make sure of the critical trick is to take a deep finesse. The commonest example occurs when declarer has nine cards of a suit missing Q J x x.

$$K\ 10\ x\ x \qquad A\ 10\ x$$
$$A\ 9\ x\ x\ x \qquad K\ 9\ x\ x\ x\ x$$

Suppose that you can afford to lose one trick, but in no circumstances two tricks. You must not lead one of the high honours, nor must you lead a low card and play an honour when the second hand has played low. Instead, you must lead low and simply cover the card played by the next player. Say that in the first example you lead low towards the dummy and West plays low; you put in the ten, and if this loses to the jack or queen the remaining cards of the suit must fall under the ace and king. If, instead, you play the king from dummy, and East shows void, you will lose two tricks to West.

An example of this safety play occurred during a match between France and Belgium in the European Championship.

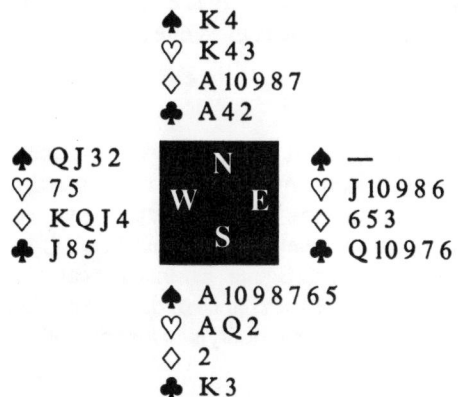

West felt very happy when his opponents reached a contract of six spades. He had an excellent lead in the king of diamonds and a very promising holding in the trump suit.

But his hopes were quickly shattered. Declarer won the first trick with the ace of diamonds, led a club to the king, and the five of spades from hand. West, of course, played low, but to his dismay South let the five run. After that, he lost just one trump trick.

No need to suppose that West was holding his cards in the middle of the table! The finesse of the five was eminently correct, because the only danger to the hand was that West, having followed to the first round, might hold all the outstanding trumps.

Note that this deep finesse with nine cards missing the queen and jack is a 'perfect' safety play, providing complete insurance against the loss of two tricks.

Example 8

You hold eight cards of a suit, with the A K 8 in one hand, the 10 in other. The object, again, is to lose at most one trick.

$$10\,x\,x\,x \qquad 10\,x\,x$$
$$A\,K\,8\,x \qquad A\,K\,8\,x\,x$$

You should begin by laying down the ace. Now, if the queen or jack or nine appears on your left, the queen or jack on your right, you follow with a low card from hand towards the 10 x x. This play saves you from losing two tricks when West has a singleton queen, jack or nine, and when East has a singleton queen or jack. It is true that in some cases, after the queen or jack has fallen, you will miss the chance to drop a doubleton QJ, losing no tricks at all; but your aim, remember, is to lose at most one trick.

Here is a typical situation in a slam contract:

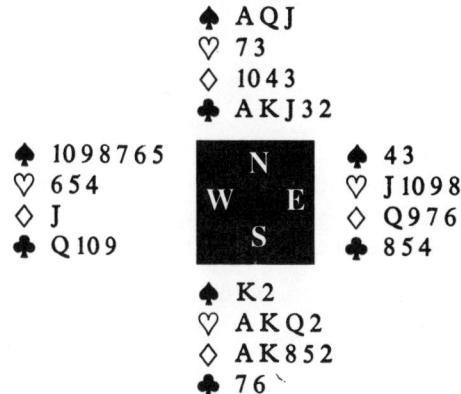

♠ A Q J
♡ 7 3
◇ 10 4 3
♣ A K J 3 2

♠ 10 9 8 7 6 5
♡ 6 5 4
◇ J
♣ Q 10 9

♠ 4 3
♡ J 10 9 8
◇ Q 9 7 6
♣ 8 5 4

♠ K 2
♡ A K Q 2
◇ A K 8 5 2
♣ 7 6

South played in six no trumps and the ten of spades was led. Four tricks in diamonds or four tricks in club would be enough for the slam, and it was natural to play on diamonds first because this was by far the stronger suit. The declarer, therefore, began with a low diamond towards the ace, on which the jack appeared from West.

South might have gone for an overtrick now by playing off the king of diamonds. Even if the queen did not fall, he would have chances to establish sufficient tricks in clubs. But there was a much safer line: a low diamond from hand could not fail to establish four tricks in the suit. The ten lost to the queen, but South then held K 8 5 over East's 9 7.

Declarer would have made the same play of a low diamond after the ace if the honour card had fallen from East, and also if West had produced the nine; this might be from J 9 or Q 9, but if the nine were single it would be a calamitous error to play off the king.

The safety play described in this section is clearly not 'perfect'. It will not succeed if either defender holds Q J 9 x (not to mention Q J 9 x x). Furthermore if it were East who held Q J 9 x, a different line of play would be more successful. But as a safety play it is still valid, because it is more likely than any other line of play to keep the losers to one.

Example 9

You and dummy hold eight or nine cards between you, missing the queen and ten. The ace and king are in different hands. Your object, as usual, is to lose not more than one trick.

K9x A Jxx KJxx
A Jxxx K9xxx A9xx

In each case you should begin with the high card in the hand that contains the jack. On the next round, if your opponent plays low, you put in the nin This line of play is proof against Q 10 x x in either defending hand.

You play the following hand in a contract of four spades:

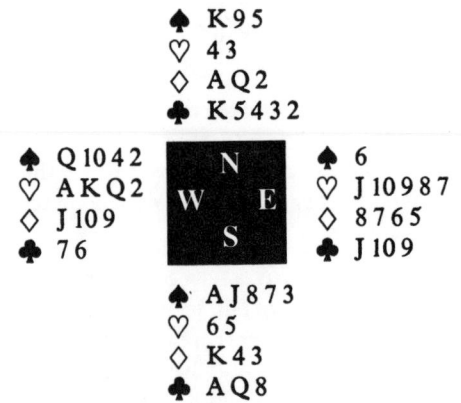

♠ K95
♡ 43
◇ AQ2
♣ K5432

♠ Q1042   ♠ 6
♡ AKQ2   ♡ J10987
◇ J109   ◇ 8765
♣ 76   ♣ J109

♠ AJ873
♡ 65
◇ K43
♣ AQ8

West begins with the king and ace of hearts, then switches to the jack of diamonds. Your only concern now is not to lose two tricks in the trump suit. You can readily afford to lose one trick, because you are 'solid' outside.

It would be a bad mistake in the circumstances to lay down the king of spades, intending to finesse the jack on the next round. That would be correct only if you needed to make all the tricks in spades.

Since you can afford to lose one trick, you adopt the regulation safety play. You lay down the ace of spades first, then lead low towards the K 9. If West showed out at this point you would go up with the king, of course. On the present occasion West plays low, whereupon you take the deep finesse of the nine. You do not mind if this loses to the queen or ten, because you will not be losing any more tricks.

This safety play is particularly valuable because, as was said at the beginning, it is proof against any 4—1 division; equally, of course, against any 4—0 division when you hold nine cards in the two hands.

Example 10

We turn next to a very simple, very common, combination of cards that is nevertheless a blind spot for more than half the bridge-playing world. You hold seven cards of a suit, including ace, king and jack, divided 4—3. Your object is to make three of the four possible tricks.

$$\begin{array}{ccc} \text{A K J x} & \text{A J x x} & \text{A x x} \\ \text{x x x} & \text{K x x} & \text{K J x x} \end{array}$$

You may think that the best chance is to cash one of the top cards, then finesse the jack, hoping either that the finesse will hold or that the suit will be divided 3—3. But that play fails when the finesse of the jack loses to a doubleton queen. The play that gives the maximum chance for three tricks is to cash both ace and king, then lead up to the J x. You win three tricks now whenever the queen is on the right side (under the jack), or the suit is divided 3—3, or *when there is a doubleton Q x over the jack.*

Most tournament players know this safety play in theory, but when the opportunity for it occurred on the following deal from a pairs contest, half the field pursued the wrong line.

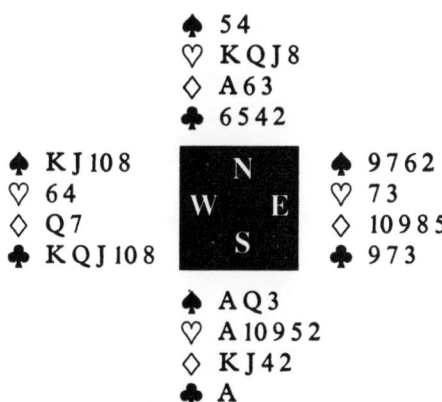

$$\spadesuit\ 5\ 4$$
$$\heartsuit\ \text{K Q J } 8$$
$$\diamondsuit\ \text{A } 6\ 3$$
$$\clubsuit\ 6\ 5\ 4\ 2$$

$$\begin{array}{ll} \spadesuit\ \text{K J } 10\ 8 & \spadesuit\ 9\ 7\ 6\ 2 \\ \heartsuit\ 6\ 4 & \heartsuit\ 7\ 3 \\ \diamondsuit\ \text{Q } 7 & \diamondsuit\ 10\ 9\ 8\ 5 \\ \clubsuit\ \text{K Q J } 10\ 8 & \clubsuit\ 9\ 7\ 3 \end{array}$$

$$\spadesuit\ \text{A Q } 3$$
$$\heartsuit\ \text{A } 10\ 9\ 5\ 2$$
$$\diamondsuit\ \text{K J } 4\ 2$$
$$\clubsuit\ \text{A}$$

The majority of the North-South pairs reached a contract of six hearts. West led the king of clubs, won by declarer's ace. All followed to two rounds of trumps.

Several players now saw the problem as 'one out of two finesses'. That is to say, they needed to find either the diamond finesse or the spade finesse, which as racing men know is a 3 to 1 on chance. It was natural to take the diamond finesse first, because if East held Q x x, South would be able to discard a spade from dummy on the thirteenth diamond and make thirteen tricks without risking the spade finesse.

This line of play proved to be ill-starred. West captured the jack of diamonds with the queen and returned a club. Sooner or later the spade finesse had to be taken, and this lost also.

The declarer who played in this fashion could claim that they were taking the best chance of making seven, but there was a better play for six. Since, after the trumps have broken 2—2, a spade discard from dummy will mean no losers in that suit, South should make the safety play in diamonds by leading king, then low to the ace. If the queen has not appeared, he leads a third round up to the J x, establishing a discard whenever East holds the queen. As the cards lie the queen appears on the second round of the suit and declarer later takes the spade finesse to try for an overtrick.

Readers who have some experience of tournament play will know that in a pairs event it is sometimes justifiable to take a slight risk in the hope of making extra tricks. Players who finessed the jack of diamonds on the present hand were quick to advance that argument. They were wrong, because six hearts is not all that easy a contract to reach; there were sure to be some pairs who would stay short of the slam. That being so, it was sensible to play six hearts as safely as possible, just as one would at rubber bridge.

Example 11

You hold nine cards of a suit, with the Q J in one hand, the A 9 in the other.

QJxx   A9x
A9xxx QJxxxx

The play with these combinations, when you can afford to lose one trick, is unexpected. The only safe play is to lead a low card away from the A 9 up to the hand containing the Q J. This is safe against K 10 8 x on either side. It is therefore a 'perfect' safety play. The problem was high-lighted on this deal from a multiple team event:

♠ Q J 7 6 2
♡ J 2
◇ A K
♣ K 5 4 3

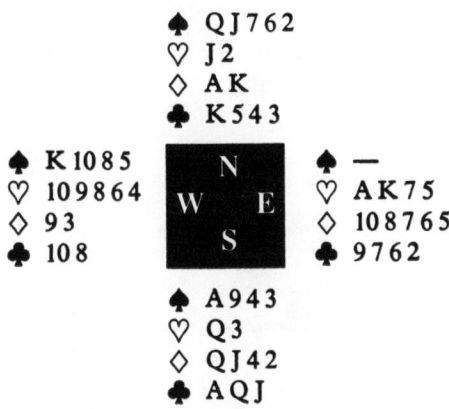

♠ K 10 8 5   ♠ —
♡ 10 9 8 6 4   ♡ A K 7 5
◇ 9 3   ◇ 10 8 7 6 5
♣ 10 8   ♣ 9 7 6 2

♠ A 9 4 3
♡ Q 3
◇ Q J 4 2
♣ A Q J

There was some 'duplication of values', as it is called, in the North-South hands, and some pairs got too high, playing in five or even six spades. There were also casualties among those who managed to stop in four spades!

The defence usually began with two tricks in hearts, followed by a diamond to dummy's king. Now in a pairs event, where overtricks are not to be spurned, it would be forgiveable to lead the queen of spades from dummy, losing no tricks in the suit when East held K x or K x x. But in any other form of scoring the correct line is to enter hand with a club and lead a low spade towards the dummy. This way, West makes only one trick with his K 10 8 5, whereas, if declarer begins with the queen from dummy, he must lose two tricks.

Now suppose that the K 10 8 5 had been held by East. West's void would have shown up on the first round and it would have been easy, after losing the first trick, to pick up the rest of the suit. Note, however, that when East has K 10 8 x it is fatal to begin with the ace.

Finally, it is *not* safe to lead low from dummy and put in the nine if East follows with a low card. Playing that way you lose two tricks foolishly when West holds the singleton 10 or K 10 x.

Example 12

You hold ten cards of a suit, including ace, queen and ten. The ace
and the queen are in opposite hands. Your object is to lose not more than
one trick.

A 10 x x	Q 10 9 x	Q x x x x
Q x x x x x	A x x x x x	A 10 x x x

You must on no account play off the ace. Instead, you lead towards
the ace, intending to put in the ten if the next opponent plays low; or,
if you are in the hand that contains the ace, you may lead low away from
this card.

Suppose you reach a contract of six hearts on the following hand:

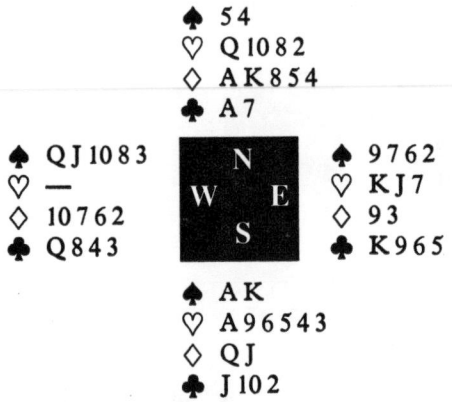

```
              ♠ 5 4
              ♡ Q 10 8 2
              ◇ A K 8 5 4
              ♣ A 7

♠ Q J 10 8 3        N        ♠ 9 7 6 2
♡ —               W   E      ♡ K J 7
◇ 10 7 6 2          S        ◇ 9 3
♣ Q 8 4 3                    ♣ K 9 6 5

              ♠ A K
              ♡ A 9 6 5 4 3
              ◇ Q J
              ♣ J 10 2
```

West leads the queen of spades, which is a little lucky for you. Had the
opening lead been a club, you would have had to win with the ace and play
a heart to the ace, hoping either to drop the king single or to dispose of your
club losers on dummy's diamonds. As it is, you have a respite. You can
afford now to lose a trump trick.

If you were on the table, you would lead a low heart, intending to cover
whatever card was played by East. However, it is not convenient to
enter dummy and your safest play is to lead a low heart from hand. When
West shows void you put in the ten, which loses to the jack. Even if East
switches to a club at this point you are in no difficulty. You win in dummy,
pick up the king of hearts by a finesse, and cash the Q J of diamonds. Then
you cross to dummy's fourth heart and discard two clubs on the A K of
diamonds.

It is easy to see that if you had led the ace of hearts from hand you
would have lost two tricks to East's K J x. The other trap with this holding
is to lead the queen from dummy; then you lose two tricks when East is
void and West has K J x.

Example 13

You hold nine cards in the two hands, missing Q J 10 x. The ace and
king are in the same hand and your object is to lose not more than one trick.

A K 9 8	A K 7	6 5 4 3
7 6 5 4 3	9 8 6 5 3 2	A K 9 8 7

You lead low towards the hand containing the A K, and if second hand
plays low you take a deep finesse. This way, you lose only one trick when
the player under the A K holds Q J 10 x.

When the following hand was played in six diamonds there was a slight
variation from the examples above, in that the missing cards were Q J 9 x.

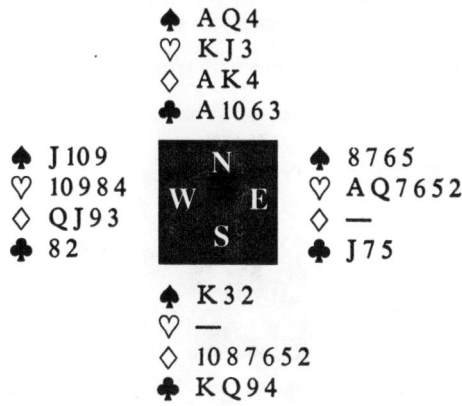

♠ A Q 4
♥ K J 3
♦ A K 4
♣ A 10 6 3

♠ J 10 9
♥ 10 9 8 4
♦ Q J 9 3
♣ 8 2

♠ 8 7 6 5
♥ A Q 7 6 5 2
♦ —
♣ J 7 5

♠ K 3 2
♥ —
♦ 10 8 7 6 5 2
♣ K Q 9 4

North, holding a balanced 21 points, opened two no trumps and South
responded three diamonds. North bid three spades to show that the
diamond response interested him, and eventually six diamonds was reached.

West led the ten of hearts, the jack was covered by the queen, and South
ruffed with the five. He then led the two of diamonds and West played the
three (it would have been a bad mistake to put in the nine). South played
the king from dummy and thereafter had to lose two trump tricks.

South was an experienced player and knew quite well that he had
carelessly omitted to make the safe (and artistic) play of finessing the four
of trumps on the first round. If he lost the trick to East, obviously the rest
of the diamonds would fall under the A K.

The only excuse that South could offer was that there might have been
a loser in clubs, and that therefore it might have been unwise to make an
exaggerated play in diamonds. But this was a feeble defence, for he would
not need to tackle clubs until the end of the play, and by that time it would
be easy to judge which, if either, defender might hold J x x x of this suit.

Example 14

You hold eight cards of a suit, with the A Q J all in the same hand. Your object, as in most safety plays, is to lose not more than one trick in the suit.

$$
\begin{array}{cc}
\text{A Q J x x} & \text{A Q J x} \\
\text{x x x} & \text{x x x x}
\end{array}
$$

The best play, assuming that sufficient entries are available to the hand opposite the A Q J, is to lay down the ace first and subsequently to lead towards the Q J x. This play saves a trick when there is a singleton king over the A Q J and it never costs; at least, it never costs the vital trick. The play is similar to Example 2, where, it will be recalled, it was right to play the ace first with A Q x x x opposite x x x.

South played the following hand in six no trumps:

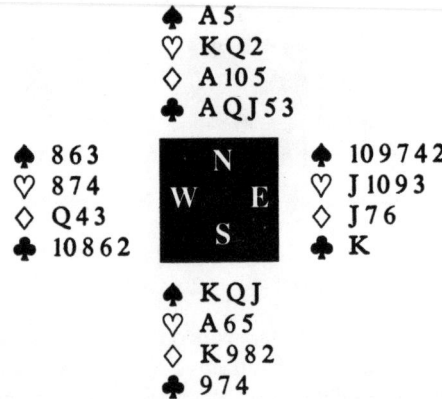

West led the eight of hearts and the declarer saw that he had eight top tricks outside the club suit. As in some circumstances it might be necessary to preserve the entries to his own hand, he won the first trick in dummy, then played off the ace of clubs. When this dropped the king he gave up a trick in clubs and made the slam.

Was this just a lucky view? Not at all! South was making a regulation safety play to guard against a singleton king. As the cards lie, it would have been fatal to take a finesse, as West would still have had a guard in clubs.

Now suppose that East had held a low singleton in clubs and West had held K 10 8 x. After cashing the ace of clubs, South would come to hand with the king of diamonds to lead a second club towards the Q J x x. West plays low (best). Declarer then crosses to the ace of hearts to play another club, establishing two more tricks in the suit. He makes as many tricks as if he had taken the finesse. Playing off the ace loses a trick when West holds K x or K x x, but that, on the present hand, would not be a vital trick.

Example 15

One important form of safety play consists of protecting a winner from
an adverse ruff. When the card in question will be equally useful later in the
play, it may be wise not to play it until trumps have been drawn. That was
the situation when the following hand was played:

♠ A 6 4 3
♡ K 5
◇ A Q 8
♣ A K 7 3

♠ 8
♡ A 4 3
◇ K J 10 9 7 2
♣ J 4 2

North-South were vulnerable and West, the dealer, opened four spades.
North doubled and East passed. Good players do not double on the strength
of trump tricks alone, so South decided to play for a vulnerable game with
a bid of five diamonds. This suited North very well, and he raised to
six diamonds.

When West led the king of spades and the dummy went down, South
reached for the ace of spades—then quickly drew his hand back. The ace of
spades might be ruffed and then there would probably be a loser in clubs
as well. Having reflected on this, the declarer played low from dummy.
East, in fact, was void of spades and held four clubs to the queen, so it
would have been fatal to play the ace of spades. When West followed with
another high spade, South ruffed in hand, drew two rounds of trumps, then
took his heart ruff. He returned to hand with another spade ruff to draw the
last trump, and the ace of spades later supplied a discard for his losing club.

The play of ducking the first spade was not too difficult here, because
of West's four-spade opening. But players do not always advertise their
long suits, and a great many contracts can be saved by refusing to allow
a winning card to be ruffed.

Examples 16 and 17

When one holds touching cards, such as K Q or J 10, and wishes to force out opposing winners, there is a natural tendency to begin the assault with one of these cards. It is a temptation that must be resisted, for unless you have a powerful sequence of touching cards it is often better to lead low on the first round. Here is a typical hand to illustrate the point:

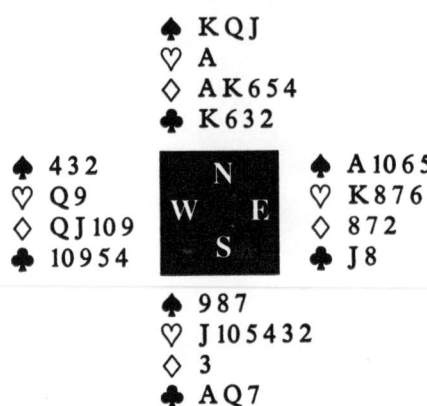

♠ K Q J
♡ A
♢ A K 6 5 4
♣ K 6 3 2

♠ 4 3 2
♡ Q 9
♢ Q J 10 9
♣ 10 9 5 4

♠ A 10 6 5
♡ K 8 7 6
♢ 8 7 2
♣ J 8

♠ 9 8 7
♡ J 10 5 4 3 2
♢ 3
♣ A Q 7

After you have rebid your modest hearts, your partner has unselfishly raised you to game in the suit. West leads the queen of diamonds and you see at once that, with one side loser in spades, you have to avoid losing three tricks in the trump suit.

You win the first trick with the ace of diamonds, cash the ace of hearts, and come to hand with the ace of clubs. The fate of the contract depends on which heart you play next. If you lead the jack or ten, West will win with the queen and you will lose two more tricks eventually to the K 8. Clearly a low heart works better, for then you retain the J 10 as equals against the king.

When a mistake of this kind is pointed out, the declarer is apt to say, 'But if I lead low I risk giving them a cheap trick with the eight or some such card.' That is an illusion. If the hearts are 3—3, South will be able to lead the suit a third time and knock the honours together, so it makes no difference whether he leads high or low on the second round. If a defender holds K Q 9 x, he will make three tricks anyway. It can *never* gain to lead the jack or ten on the second round.

Here is another deal that exhibits the same principle:

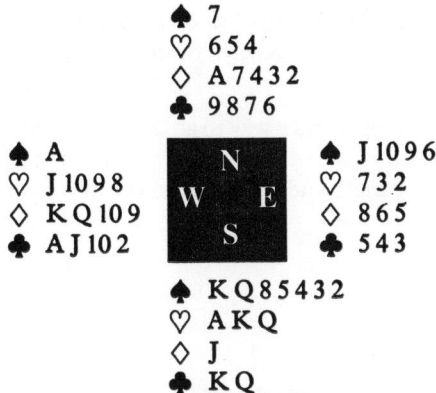

             ♠ 7
             ♡ 6 5 4
             ◇ A 7 4 3 2
             ♣ 9 8 7 6

♠ A   ♠ J 10 9 6
♡ J 10 9 8   ♡ 7 3 2
◇ K Q 10 9   ◇ 8 6 5
♣ A J 10 2   ♣ 5 4 3

             ♠ K Q 8 5 4 3 2
             ♡ A K Q
             ◇ J
             ♣ K Q

South opened two spades, forcing for one round, and finished in four spades. West led the king of diamonds, won by dummy's ace. On the seven of spades East played the ten, quite a wily card.

South might have played East for A 10 alone, but he knew his safety plays and had the self-discipline to play low from hand. West's ace now captured nothing of value and the defence made just one more trump and the ace of clubs.

A little experimenting will show that when the object is to lose not more than two tricks with this combination, to play the king or queen on the first round cannot gain. If East had held, say, A J 10, he would have made a trick with the ten and later a trick with the ace—exactly the same as if South had played the king on the ten and returned a low one.

Example 18

It quite often happens that a relatively low card, such as the nine, will help to establish tricks in a suit even when the opposite hand contains the A K Q 10.

A declarer at rubber bridge found a way to go down in three no trumps on the deal below. No abstruse safety play was required; all that was needed was to count the tricks and, as it were, make use of all the troops available.

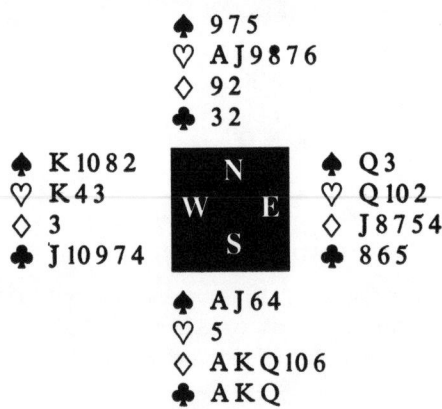

```
                    ♠ 975
                    ♡ A J 9 8 7 6
                    ◇ 92
                    ♣ 32

  ♠ K 10 8 2                      ♠ Q 3
  ♡ K 4 3         N               ♡ Q 10 2
  ◇ 3          W     E            ◇ J 8 7 5 4
  ♣ J 10 9 7 4      S             ♣ 8 6 5

                    ♠ A J 6 4
                    ♡ 5
                    ◇ A K Q 10 6
                    ♣ A K Q
```

South opened with a conventional two clubs and North responded two hearts, which in the system showed simply the ace of hearts. South bid three diamonds and North three hearts. Now South sensibly bid three no trumps; had he chosen three spades, the partnership would have gone past the best contract.

West led the jack of clubs against three no trumps, and South's opening manoeuvre was to lay down the ace and king of diamonds. Goodbye to the game! East now had a double stop in diamonds and the declarer was held to eight tricks.

It is easy to see that South could have ensured four tricks in diamonds by giving up a trick to the jack. He can play off the ace of diamonds first, because the jack might be single; when this card does not appear, he should follow with a low diamond to the nine.

There are many similar situations where the safest way to establish an extra trick is to make full use of the low cards. For example:

1) 9 8
   K Q J 4 2

2) 10 3
   A K Q 8 5 2

With the cards in the first diagram, South can make sure of three tricks by running the eight. If he makes the normal play of leading up to the K Q J 6 4 and playing an honour, he will make only two tricks when either defender holds A 10 7 x x, or when West holds the singleton ace. In the second example low from hand ensures five tricks against J 9 x x x on either side.

Example 19

Many forms of safety play are easy to execute so long as you know the type and are on your guard. But when you meet them for the first time in your career you may go wrong if you have not been warned. One of the authors misplayed the following hand in his youth, but has not made the same mistake since!

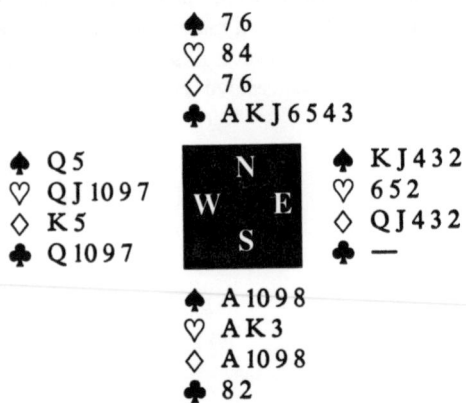

```
                    ♠ 7 6
                    ♡ 8 4
                    ◇ 7 6
                    ♣ A K J 6 5 4 3
  ♠ Q 5                              ♠ K J 4 3 2
  ♡ Q J 10 9 7          N           ♡ 6 5 2
  ◇ K 5           W         E       ◇ Q J 4 3 2
  ♣ Q 10 9 7           S            ♣ —
                    ♠ A 10 9 8
                    ♡ A K 3
                    ◇ A 10 9 8
                    ♣ 8 2
```

The contract was three no trumps and West led the queen of hearts. South won and led a low club, on which West inserted the ten and dummy the jack. East showed out and South suddenly found himself making just three tricks in clubs instead of six. He went two down in the vulnerable game instead of making an overtrick.

The safe play, of course, was to duck in dummy on the first round of clubs. If East follows suit, the rest of the clubs must be good, and if East shows void, it is simple to take a finesse later against West's guarded queen. The club situation on this deal gives rise to a very pretty deceptive play. Suppose West, on the first round of clubs, puts in the *queen*! Then it would take a very careful player indeed in the South chair not to cover with the king.

Example 20

In the safety plays that have been discussed so far we have always assumed that the declarer has no entry problems and that he can go freely from hand to hand to make the necessary leads. At the table it is often not like that at all. The essence of many safety plays is that the declarer foresees an entry problem and sacrifices a possible trick to overcome it.

As South, you play the following hand in three no trumps:

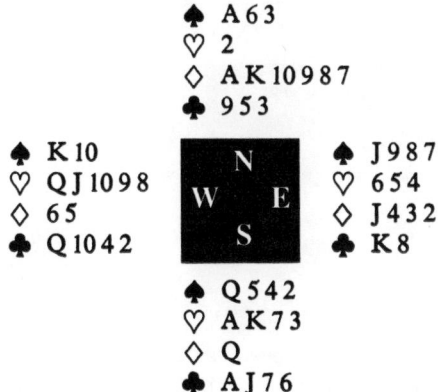

```
              ♠ A 6 3
              ♡ 2
              ◇ A K 10 9 8 7
              ♣ 9 5 3
  ♠ K 10                          ♠ J 9 8 7
  ♡ Q J 10 9 8      N             ♡ 6 5 4
  ◇ 6 5          W     E          ◇ J 4 3 2
  ♣ Q 10 4 2        S             ♣ K 8
              ♠ Q 5 4 2
              ♡ A K 7 3
              ◇ Q
              ♣ A J 7 6
```

West leads the queen of hearts from his strong sequence, and your first problem is whether to capture this trick or hold up. On the whole it is better to win, because a spade switch could be awkward; you would have to play low from dummy and East might be able to win and shift to clubs.

You win the first heart, therefore, and lead the queen of diamonds, on which West play low. This is the critical moment. If you fail to overtake, you have to use the ace of spades to enter dummy, and then, if the jack of diamonds does not fall under the A K, you will not be able to bring in the rest of the suit.

Since five diamonds will be enough for your contract you make the safety play of overtaking the queen with the king. Then you force out the jack and the ace of spades is still there as an entry.

Example 21

The next hand has the same general theme: the declarer makes an
unusual play to preserve the entry for a long suit. But this time it is done
not by overtaking a high card, but by refusing to part with an entry, at the
cost of an obvious trick.

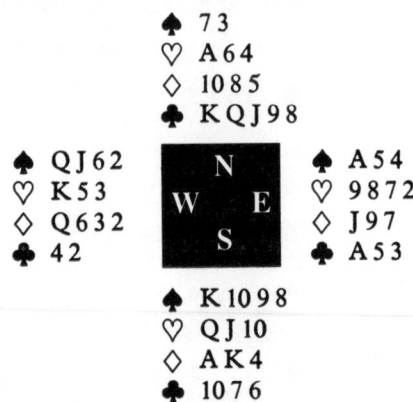

```
                    ♠ 7 3
                    ♡ A 6 4
                    ◇ 10 8 5
                    ♣ K Q J 9 8
  ♠ Q J 6 2          N          ♠ A 5 4
  ♡ K 5 3        W       E       ♡ 9 8 7 2
  ◇ Q 6 3 2          S          ◇ J 9 7
  ♣ 4 2                          ♣ A 5 3
                    ♠ K 10 9 8
                    ♡ Q J 10
                    ◇ A K 4
                    ♣ 10 7 6
```

North opened with a sub-standard one club, justified perhaps by the
good suit, and South responded three no trumps, which was passed out.
West led the two of spades and East won with the ace.

After some thought East returned the nine of hearts. This was good play
on his part. West's lead of the two of spades suggested a suit of four cards
only, so there was little future there. More important was to drive out the
ace of hearts, which would be an entry for the clubs, once this suit has
been established.

South covered the nine of hearts with the ten and West played the
king. This presented the declarer with the chance of making three tricks in
hearts, but nevertheless he played low from dummy. West returned a
heart, won by the jack. Now South set about the clubs. East won the third
round and led a spade. South took the king, entered dummy with the ace of
hearts, and cashed the remaining clubs. Thus he made game with four
clubs, two diamonds, two hearts and one spade.

It is clear that if South had parted with the ace of hearts on the first round
of the suit, he would have had no entry for the long clubs.

Example 22

There is opportunity sometimes to make two safety plays in the same suit. A card that would be wrong on the first round becomes right on the second round. Observe South's management of the spade suit on the following deal:

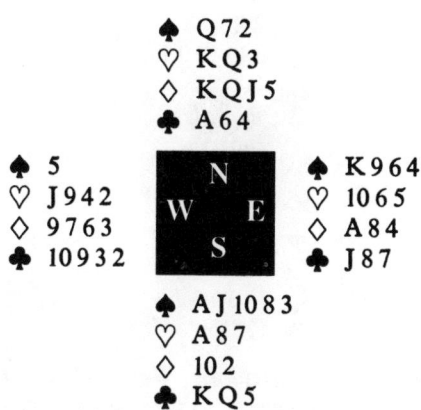

```
                    ♠ Q 7 2
                    ♡ K Q 3
                    ◇ K Q J 5
                    ♣ A 6 4
   ♠ 5                            ♠ K 9 6 4
   ♡ J 9 4 2          N           ♡ 10 6 5
   ◇ 9 7 6 3      W       E       ◇ A 8 4
   ♣ 10 9 3 2         S           ♣ J 8 7
                    ♠ A J 10 8 3
                    ♡ A 8 7
                    ◇ 10 2
                    ♣ K Q 5
```

Bidding with plenty of spirit, North-South arrived at a contract of six spades. West led the two of clubs and declarer was in dummy. As the ace of diamonds was a certain loser, it was clear that South needed to pick up the trump suit without loss.

As declarer, would you begin with a low spade from dummy or with the queen? On the present hand it would make no difference, but in some cases the queen would be a mistake. Suppose that East held the singleton king; then a lead of the queen would establish a trick for West's 9 x x x.

Following the general principle, therefore, of leading low for a finesse unless a solid sequence is held, South began with the two of spades from dummy. West played the four and the jack held the trick. South then entered dummy with a heart for a second lead of spades.

Whereas the queen would have been a mistake on the first round, now it is correct. East will probably cover with the king; then South crosses to dummy again in hearts and finesses against East's 9 x of spades.

If declarer leads the seven of spades from dummy on the second round he can hardly let it run without second sight. He puts in the ten from hand, but then East's K 9 wins a certain trick.

Examples 23 and 24

On many hands safety consists of losing the lead (if at all) to one opponent rather than the other. The two deals that follow illustrate that point.

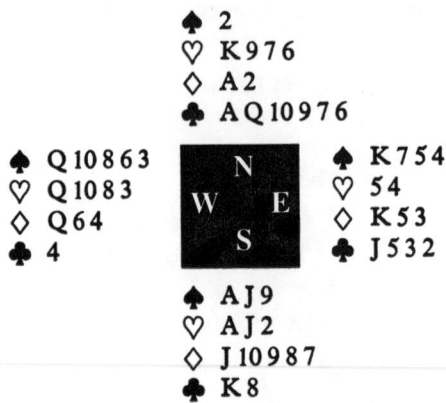

You are South, playing in three no trumps. West leads the six of spades and East plays the king. As you have a chance of second trick with the J 9, you win with the ace.

Counting your tricks, you see that you have four certain winners outside the clubs. Thus five tricks in clubs will be enough for game. The only danger lies in a spade lead from East through your J 9.

To avert this danger you decide to establish the clubs without giving East a chance to gain the lead. You cross to dummy with the king of hearts and lead a low club. When East plays low, you put in the eight. As it happens, the eight holds the trick. You then cash the king, cross to the ace of diamonds, and run the rest of the clubs.

You would not have minded if the eight of clubs had lost to the jack in West's hand, because no attack by West would cause you any problem. If he switched to diamonds, for example, you would go up with the ace and lead the ace of clubs, dropping your king beneath it.

In the last example your unusual play of the club suit was caused by the vulnerable holding in spades. On the next hand there is a question of timing. It is not safe to allow East to win the first trick, because he may probe a weak spot in another suit.

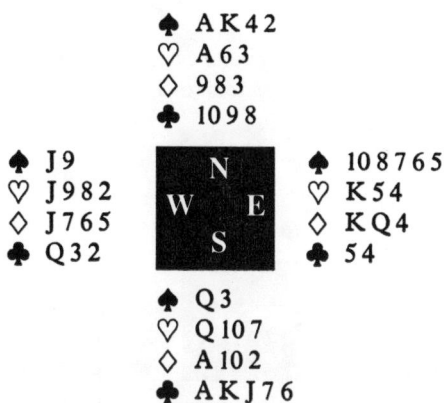

```
              ♠ A K 4 2
              ♡ A 6 3
              ◇ 9 8 3
              ♣ 10 9 8
  ♠ J 9                      ♠ 10 8 7 6 5
  ♡ J 9 8 2      N            ♡ K 5 4
  ◇ J 7 6 5   W     E         ◇ K Q 4
  ♣ Q 3 2       S            ♣ 5 4
              ♠ Q 3
              ♡ Q 10 7
              ◇ A 10 2
              ♣ A K J 7 6
```

South was in three no trumps and West led the two of hearts. Declarer could be sure of two tricks in hearts by playing low from dummy, but he realized there was a danger in this line; East might be able to win with the king of hearts and switch to diamonds.

South made the excellent play, therefore, of going up with the ace of hearts and finessing the ten of clubs. West won this trick and switched to diamonds, but the game was safe now. South won the first diamond to avoid the danger of a lead through his Q 10 of hearts. He had nine sure tricks by way of four clubs, three spades, and two red aces.

If declarer had played low from dummy on the first round of hearts, East would have won with the king and might well have switched to the king of diamonds. South can make the contract if he does everything right (he must take the second diamond, then play three rounds of spades, giving West an awkward discard), but in practice he would probably take the club finesse sooner or later.

Example 25

An ace will (usually) win a trick and will sometimes furnish an invaluable discard. If these two functions can be combined, the profit will be the greater.

The following hand was played in a pairs event before the stratagem used by the declarer was as well known as it is to-day.

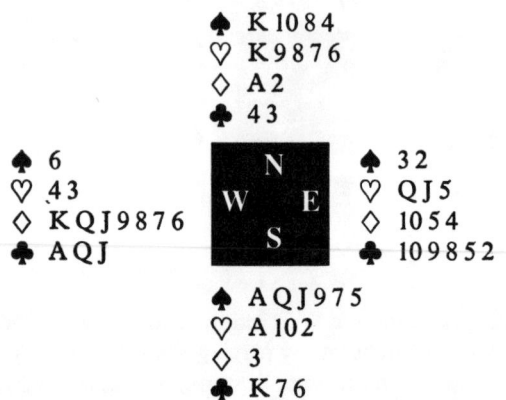

```
              ♠ K 10 8 4
              ♡ K 9 8 7 6
              ◇ A 2
              ♣ 4 3
  ♠ 6                        ♠ 3 2
  ♡ 4 3          N           ♡ Q J 5
  ◇ K Q J 9 8 7 6   W   E     ◇ 10 5 4
  ♣ A Q J          S         ♣ 10 9 8 5 2
              ♠ A Q J 9 7 5
              ♡ A 10 2
              ◇ 3
              ♣ K 7 6
```

North-South were vulnerable, and in face of determined defence by West they went to five spades over five diamonds. All passed and West made the normal lead of the king of diamonds.

South would have enough tricks if he could establish the hearts, but in doing this he might lose the lead to East, who would hasten to play a club through the king. A reasonable plan for declarer would be to win with the ace of diamonds, draw trumps, and lead a low heart from the table, hoping to duck the trick into West's hand. This line fails because East has both queen and jack of hearts and will no doubt play one of them when the low card is led from dummy.

South can improve his chances considerably by the clever play of ducking the first round of diamonds. If West continues diamonds, he discards a heart from hand, draws trumps, then plays off ace and king of hearts. When all follow, he ruffs the third round (remember he has disposed of a heart on the ace of diamonds), returns to dummy with a trump, and makes two more heart tricks, discarding clubs from hand. He loses just one diamond and one club.

Example 26

Many forms of safety play are directed towards retaining control in a suit contract. Every player knows that it can be disastrous to arrive at a point where a defender has more trumps than the declarer. The following hand illustrates one way of avoiding that situation.

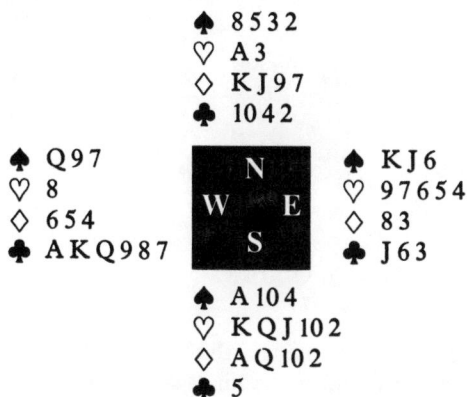

```
            ♠ 8 5 3 2
            ♡ A 3
            ◇ K J 9 7
            ♣ 10 4 2

♠ Q 9 7                      ♠ K J 6
♡ 8            N             ♡ 9 7 6 5 4
◇ 6 5 4     W     E          ◇ 8 3
♣ A K Q 9 8 7    S           ♣ J 6 3

            ♠ A 10 4
            ♡ K Q J 10 2
            ◇ A Q 10 2
            ♣ 5
```

South is in four hearts. West leads the king of clubs and follows with the ace.

The contract (so long as you haven't looked at the opposing hands) seems safe enough. Why not ruff, draw the trumps, and run the diamonds, making nine tricks in the red suits plus the ace of spades ?

See what happens if declarer follows that line. West shows out on the second trump, and when declarer turns to diamonds (better than drawing two more trumps) East ruffs the third round and plays another club. After South has ruffed this, East has yet another trump trick to come, plus two tricks in spades.

The safe play, guarding against five trumps in one hand, is to discard losing spades on the second and third rounds of clubs. If West leads yet a fourth club, South ruffs low in dummy and has no difficulty in making the rest of the tricks.

Example 27

The same sort of problem arises on the next hand, but now there are more complications in the play.

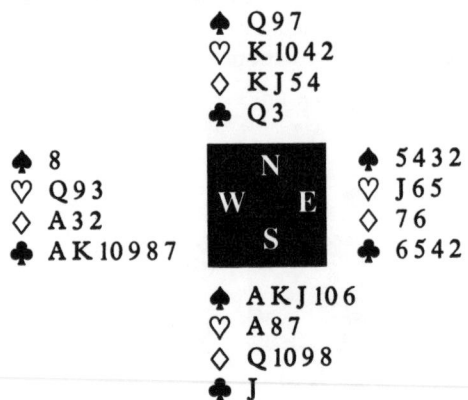

South is in four spades and West begins with two top clubs. Let us suppose that South ruffs and draws two rounds of trumps, discovering West's singleton. He can draw the rest of the trumps all right, but it will take all his own trumps to do so, and he still has not forced out the ace of diamonds.

The best plan, therefore, after two rounds of trumps, would be to switch to diamonds. If West could be persuaded to part with his ace of diamonds on the first round, declarer's problems would be over, as dummy could take care of any future club lead. But a good player in West's position would hold up the ace of diamonds on the first round. He would win the second round and give his partner a ruff. East would exit with his last trump, and South would eventually lose a fourth trick in hearts.

These troubles are avoided if South, recognizing that his control of the trump situation is open to attack, declines to ruff the second club, discarding a heart. It is true that there is a slight risk that the diamonds may be 4—1 and that the defenders will take an immediate ruff, but the danger of that is much less than of losing trump control. (If West had held a low singleton in diamonds he might well have led it, and if he has A x x x he may not find the switch.)

Examples 28, 29 and 30

In the last two examples the declarer declined to ruff in his own hand, so that the dummy could eventually take care of the dangerous suit. The same purpose can be achieved by giving up a trump trick early on when there is a likely, or even possible, loser in the trump suit. Then, as before, dummy can take the force and declarer does not weaken his own trump length. The three examples below are all examples of this type of play; after studying them, you will not fail to recognize similar hands at the table.

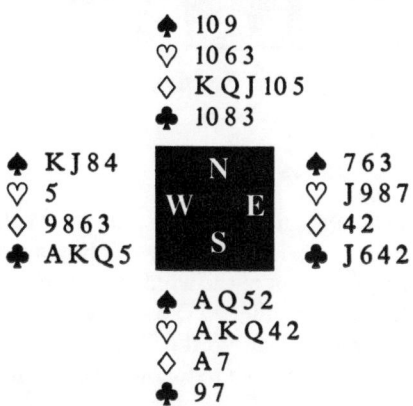

```
              ♠ 10 9
              ♡ 10 6 3
              ◇ K Q J 10 5
              ♣ 10 8 3
♠ K J 8 4         N          ♠ 7 6 3
♡ 5          W        E      ♡ J 9 8 7
◇ 9 8 6 3         S          ◇ 4 2
♣ A K Q 5                    ♣ J 6 4 2
              ♠ A Q 5 2
              ♡ A K Q 4 2
              ◇ A 7
              ♣ 9 7
```

South plays in four hearts after West opened one club. The defence begins with three rounds of clubs. Suppose that South ruffs and draws two rounds of trumps, discovering West's singleton. He cannot force out East's winning trump, because East will then make the setting trick in clubs; and the spade finesse is likely to be wrong because West has opened the bidding.

South's best chance is to test the diamonds, hoping that East will follow to four rounds; but alas, East ruffs the third round and exits with a trump. The contract will now be defeated by two tricks.

It would not help South on this occasion to refuse to ruff the third club. Having ruffed the club, he should reflect that he can afford to lose a trick in hearts, and he must aim to lose it while there is still a trump in dummy. So he plays off ace of hearts and follows with a *low* one. East wins and cannot effectively play a club because there is still a trump in dummy. East will probably exit with a spade. South goes up with the ace, draws the remaining trumps, and runs his five diamond tricks without any unseemly interruption.

Having studied that hand, you won't go wrong on the next one:

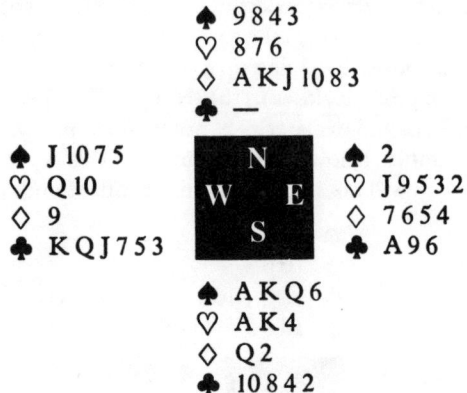

```
                    ♠ 9 8 4 3
                    ♡ 8 7 6
                    ◇ A K J 10 8 3
                    ♣ —
  ♠ J 10 7 5              N          ♠ 2
  ♡ Q 10            W          E     ♡ J 9 5 3 2
  ◇ 9                     S          ◇ 7 6 5 4
  ♣ K Q J 7 5 3                      ♣ A 9 6
                    ♠ A K Q 6
                    ♡ A K 4
                    ◇ Q 2
                    ♣ 10 8 4 2
```

West leads the king of clubs against six spades. Declarer ruffs in dummy and plays a spade to the ace, to which all follow. If he plays another high trump, the contract disappears out of the window. Dummy at this stage will have only one trump left, South will hold Q 6 and West J 10. South may ruff a club and turn to diamonds, but West will ruff the second round and cash two more club tricks, with a heart to follow at the finish.

South should give up his trump trick on the second, or even the first round. Then there will still be a trump in dummy to take care of a club from West. Contract made instead of down three!

The third hand is similar, but perhaps a little more difficult because now it is essential to make the safety play on the very first round of trumps.

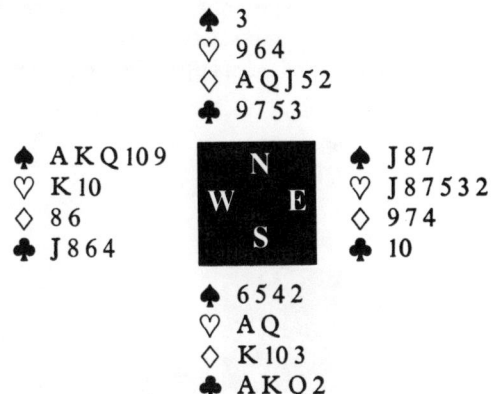

```
                  ♠ 3
                  ♡ 9 6 4
                  ◇ A Q J 5 2
                  ♣ 9 7 5 3
♠ A K Q 10 9                    ♠ J 8 7
♡ K 10          N              ♡ J 8 7 5 3 2
◇ 8 6        W     E           ◇ 9 7 4
♣ J 8 6 4       S              ♣ 10
                  ♠ 6 5 4 2
                  ♡ A Q
                  ◇ K 10 3
                  ♣ A K Q 2
```

North-South did well to finish in five clubs, the only game contract that had a chance. West won the first trick with the king of spades, and after some consideration led a diamond to the second trick. If South had held only two diamonds, this would have been a fine defence, as a second diamond would cut the declarer away from dummy's suit.

As it was, South won the diamond switch with the king, ruffed a spade, and led a trump from dummy. East played the ten and was allowed to hold the trick! Now everything was under control. South won the heart return, ruffed another spade, drew trumps, and ran off the diamonds, making game with three top trumps, two ruffs, ace of hearts, and five diamonds.

Let us see what would have happened if South had ducked the second round of clubs instead of the first. West would have won and promptly returned a trump, removing the last club from dummy (South has already ruffed a spade, remember). That would have left South one trick short. He needed two spade ruffs, and the only safe way to negotiate them was to ruff a spade at the first opportunity, then give up the first round of trumps.

Example 31

One of the commonest forms of play consists of taking a ruff in the short trump hand, thus increasing the number of tricks that can be won in the trump suit. In this area, too, various safety plays can be employed to increase the chance of a ruff. Two of them appear in the following hand from a pairs event.

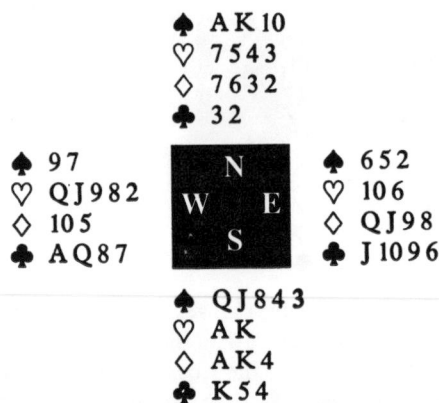

	♠ A K 10
	♡ 7 5 4 3
	◇ 7 6 3 2
	♣ 3 2

♠ 9 7		♠ 6 5 2
♡ Q J 9 8 2		♡ 10 6
◇ 10 5		◇ Q J 9 8
♣ A Q 8 7		♣ J 10 9 6

	♠ Q J 8 4 3
	♡ A K
	◇ A K 4
	♣ K 5 4

The best contract for North-South is three no trumps, but a number of pairs finished in four spades. The usual lead against four spades was the queen of hearts, won by the declarer's ace.

Counting his tricks in a spade contract, South can see five in the trump suit plus two A K's. There is an excellent chance to establish a tenth trick by ruffing the third round of clubs, and the cautious declarers set about this at once by leading a club from hand at trick two. Whatever the return, declarer played another round of clubs and could not be prevented from ruffing the third round.

Nevertheless, some players were defeated in four spades. After winning the first heart they crossed to dummy with a trump and optimistically led a club towards the king. West took the ace and promptly switched to trumps. As one round of trumps had been played already, the result was that South was unable to ruff any club at all, for naturally East won the next round of clubs and knocked out the third trump!

At one table the declarer had to contend with an opening lead of trumps. This appears to ruin his hopes of club ruff, but he still made the contract by cleverly taking advantage of a genuine 'half chance'.

In dummy at trick one South led a club, on which East played the jack. If the king of clubs was over the ace, it would provide a tenth trick anyway, so for the moment South played low. East followed his partner's defence by returning a trump to dummy. When East played the ten on the next round of clubs, South covered with the king, forcing West to take the trick. Luck was with him, as West had no more trumps to lead. Thus South was able to develop his tenth trick by ruffing the third club in dummy.

Example 32

We have seen in previous examples that many safety plays are designed to retain communication between the two hands; often a trick that could easily be won is surrendered for this purpose.

The deal below shows a slightly different situation: a trick is surrendered, not to retain an entry card, but to create one.

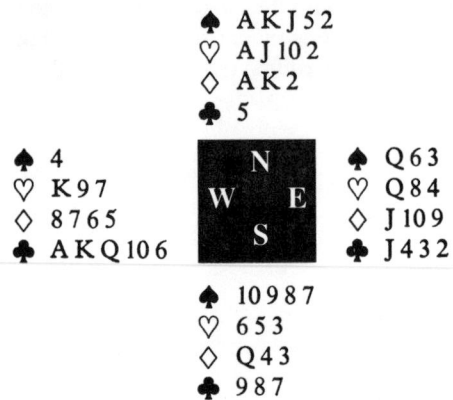

```
                    ♠ A K J 5 2
                    ♡ A J 10 2
                    ◇ A K 2
                    ♣ 5
    ♠ 4                          ♠ Q 6 3
    ♡ K 9 7         N            ♡ Q 8 4
    ◇ 8 7 6 5    W     E         ◇ J 10 9
    ♣ A K Q 10 6    S            ♣ J 4 3 2
                    ♠ 10 9 8 7
                    ♡ 6 5 3
                    ◇ Q 4 3
                    ♣ 9 8 7
```

West opens one club, North doubles, and after a pass by East South responds one spade. North raises to four spades and all pass. West leads the king of clubs and follows with a second club, forcing dummy to ruff.

It may seem that the natural play is to lead out ace and king of spades. If the queen falls, South will have enough entries to hand to finesse hearts twice. If, at worst, the ace and king of spades do not bring down the queen, declarer can try leading the jack of hearts from dummy; this will be good enough if West has K Q x, because South will later come to hand with the queen of diamonds and pick up the rest of the heart suit by a finesse.

It can be seen that as the cards lie this play will not succeed. After ace and king of spades declarer leads the jack of hearts from dummy, losing to West's king; when the heart finesse is taken later, it loses to the queen.

So, what can be done? The answer is that, lacking entries to hand, but able to afford the loss of one trump trick, South should play off ace of spades at trick three and then follow with the *jack* of spades. East makes his queen and, we will say, exits with a club. South is careful to ruff this with a high trump in dummy; then he draws the outstanding trump with the ten and leads a heart, finessing the jack and losing to the queen. He will regain the lead later with the queen of diamonds, and a second finesse of hearts will win the contract.

You will find it useful to play this hand over two or three times, for it contains a valuable lesson in the care and management of entries.

Example 33

In any no trump contract it is normal and necessary for the declarer to pay special attention to the suit led. He should ask himself in particular: 'How many cards does the leader hold? What are the dangers in this suit and how can they be met?'

Here is an example of a contract thrown away because the declarer failed to make these calculations:

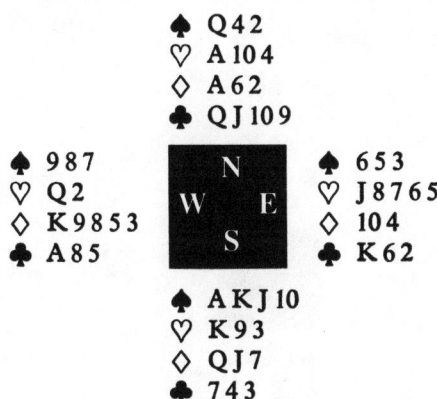

```
              ♠ Q 4 2
              ♡ A 10 4
              ◇ A 6 2
              ♣ Q J 10 9

♠ 9 8 7            N            ♠ 6 5 3
♡ Q 2         W        E       ♡ J 8 7 6 5
◇ K 9 8 5 3       S            ◇ 10 4
♣ A 8 5                        ♣ K 6 2

              ♠ A K J 10
              ♡ K 9 3
              ◇ Q J 7
              ♣ 7 4 3
```

South was in three no trumps and West led the five of diamonds. The two was played from dummy and the ten by East. South won and ...

You're right! Natural as it seemed to head the ten with the queen, it was the wrong play here, as the sequel soon showed. Aware, perhaps, that he had already made a mistake, South tried to recover by crossing to dummy with a spade and leading the nine of clubs from the table. East did very well to put on the king, thus protecting his partner's entry. Now a diamond was led through South's J 7. Declarer won the third round in dummy, but his fears were confirmed when West won the next club and defeated the contract with two more diamond tricks.

The main danger to this contract was that West might hold five diamonds and one of the club honours. Suppose that South plays low on the first lead (as no doubt he would have done had he held K x x instead of Q J x). East leads a second diamond, but when he comes in with the king of clubs he cannot clear the suit.

It is true that playing the queen of diamonds on the first trick would be right if West held both ace and king of clubs; but that, obviously, is against the odds.

Example 34

On many hands played in a suit contract the declarer has to choose whether
to play a 'ruffing game', planning to ruff losers in dummy, or to play for
'suit establishment'—drawing trumps and then running a long suit.
Which course is better cannot be judged in advance of individual
circumstances, but this much can be said in advance: when the choice
appears to be close, the suit establishment game tends to be better, because
the declarer has more chances to overcome a bad trump division.

The following hand is a typical example:

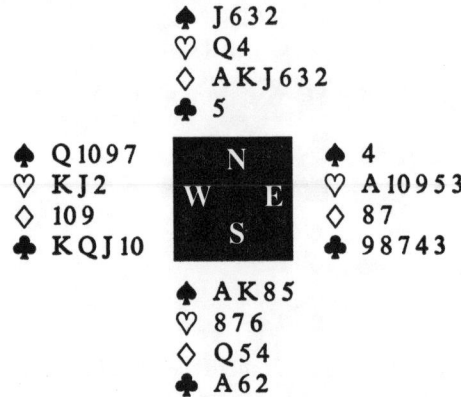

```
                    ♠ J 6 3 2
                    ♡ Q 4
                    ◇ A K J 6 3 2
                    ♣ 5
    ♠ Q 10 9 7         N         ♠ 4
    ♡ K J 2                      ♡ A 10 9 5 3
    ◇ 10 9        W       E      ◇ 8 7
    ♣ K Q J 10        S          ♣ 9 8 7 4 3
                    ♠ A K 8 5
                    ♡ 8 7 6
                    ◇ Q 5 4
                    ♣ A 6 2
```

South is in four spades and West leads the king of clubs. It is
interesting to consider how players of three different grades would tackle
this problem.

That legendary character, Mrs Guggenheim, who could never resist
'ruffing in', would win with the ace of clubs and hastily ruff a club.
Returning to hand with the ace of spades, she would ruff another club, then
play dummy's last spade to the king. Now, even if the trumps were 3—2,
she would be in difficulties, having three heart losers: she would need, in
effect, the hand with the outstanding trump to hold at least three diamonds.

A better player would not dream of weakening the dummy by ruffing. He (or she) would win the club lead and play off ace and king of spades, then play on diamonds, making the contract very easily whenever the spades were 3—2. But on the present occasion that line would fail. If South followed with a third spade, West would go up with the queen and play a club, forcing dummy to ruff with the jack of spades and establishing a trick for his ten. Alternatively, South might turn to diamonds after two rounds of trumps; then West would ruff the third diamond, cash the queen of spades, and take two tricks in hearts.

Finally, an expert in safety manoeuvres would recognize that the contract could be made not only when trumps were 3—2, but also when West held Q 10 x x. He would play ace of spades, then a low spade. West cannot do better than go up with the queen, take two hearts, then exit with a club, which dummy ruffs. Now declarer cashes the jack of spades, returns to hand with the queen of diamonds to draw the outstanding trump, and discards his remaining losers on dummy's diamond suit.

Example 35

Some players, like Mrs Guggenheim in the preceding example, are very
fond of making low trumps by ruffing; others have a strong fancy for
finesses, whose successful accomplishment seems to give them a feeling of
superiority. On the following deal both tendencies had to be resisted, for
better safety. It occurred in a mixed pairs event and was excellently
handled by the partner of one of the authors.

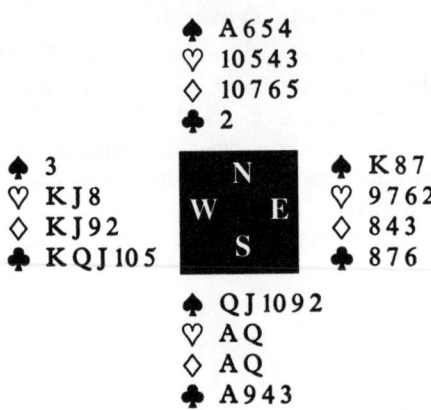

```
                    ♠ A 6 5 4
                    ♡ 10 5 4 3
                    ◊ 10 7 6 5
                    ♣ 2
    ♠ 3                           ♠ K 8 7
    ♡ K J 8            N          ♡ 9 7 6 2
    ◊ K J 9 2       W     E       ◊ 8 4 3
    ♣ K Q J 10 5       S          ♣ 8 7 6
                    ♠ Q J 10 9 2
                    ♡ A Q
                    ◊ A Q
                    ♣ A 9 4 3
```

South played in four spades and West, who had made a take-out double
of the opening one spade, led the king of clubs.

Three finesses were offered, but South took none of them! This was
her line of play:

Win with ace of clubs, ruff a club with a low trump; return to ace of
hearts, ruff another club low; return to ace of diamonds, ruff the next club
with the ace of spades; lead a spade and lose just the three kings.

You may think that it would not have been particularly dangerous to
finesse in one of the red suits, but observe the consequence of doing that.
West wins and promptly leads his singleton trump. South may go up with
dummy's ace, but when she tries to ruff the fourth round of clubs she is
overruffed by East's eight of spades. The only safe line was the one she
followed.

Example 36

We saw several hands earlier on where the declarer refused to ruff in his own hand in order to protect his length in trumps. Occasionally a rather different situation occurs: declarer refuses to ruff in dummy, the hand with the shorter trumps, so as to retain an entry for dummy's side suit. Here is an example of this comparatively rare situation:

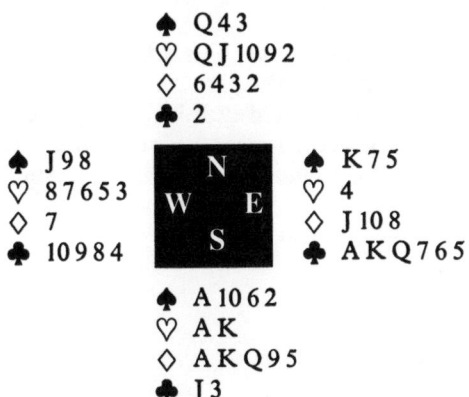

```
              ♠ Q 4 3
              ♡ Q J 10 9 2
              ◇ 6 4 3 2
              ♣ 2

♠ J 9 8          N          ♠ K 7 5
♡ 8 7 6 5 3   W     E       ♡ 4
◇ 7              S          ◇ J 10 8
♣ 10 9 8 4                  ♣ A K Q 7 6 5

              ♠ A 10 6 2
              ♡ A K
              ◇ A K Q 9 5
              ♣ J 3
```

South played in five diamonds after East had overcalled in clubs. West led the ten of clubs, won by East's queen. Most players in East's position would be attracted by the singleton heart, but East was sure that South held the ace of hearts and played the stronger defence of leading a second club, with a view to forcing the dummy. South ruffed and drew two rounds of trumps, but from that point of trumps, but from that point the hand went sour. He drew the third trump, cashed ace and king of hearts, then led a low spade to the queen and king. East returned a spade and another trick had to be lost.

Despite the excellent defence, South could have made his contract by a clever counterstroke. Instead of ruffing the second club, he discards a spade from dummy. If East plays a third club, South ruffs with the nine, draws trumps, cashes the top hearts, and enters dummy by leading the five of diamonds to dummy's six.

Example 37

Nobody who was investing his capital would be satisfied with the possibility of a 10% return on his money when there was a chance of losing the entire amount.

Similarly, at bridge, it is silly to risk any contract, and particularly a slam contract, for the sake of a possible overtrick (worth a good deal less than 10% of the amount at stake).

One of the authors was partnered at rubber bridge by a player who was in the habit of 'shaving an egg' when he played bridge: he would always capture a trick with the smallest card available, despite the risk of blocking a suit or being unable to give his partner the lead. The rubber on this occasion went very well for a while, but all good things come to an end.

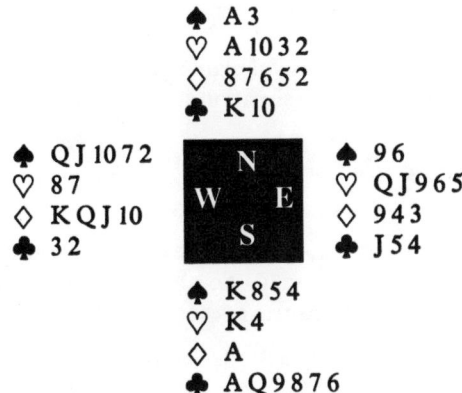

♠ A 3
♡ A 10 3 2
◇ 8 7 6 5 2
♣ K 10

♠ Q J 10 7 2
♡ 8 7
◇ K Q J 10
♣ 3 2

♠ 9 6
♡ Q J 9 6 5
◇ 9 4 3
♣ J 5 4

♠ K 8 5 4
♡ K 4
◇ A
♣ A Q 9 8 7 6

South opened one club; North, not caring to introduce his flimsy diamond suit, responded one heart; and South rebid three clubs. This, perhaps, was not quite in the modern style—one spade would be more fashionable—but it was a fair expression of South's values. North now jumped to six clubs, expecting this contract to present no difficulty.

West led the king of diamonds against six clubs. South judged correctly that the best plan would be to ruff two spades in dummy. He began with a spade to the ace, led back a spade to the king, then played a third round, ruffing with dummy's ten of clubs. East overruffed with the jack and returned a trump to dummy's king. Now there was no parking-place for the fourth spade.

This was a scandalous disregard of the safety regulations! The contract could hardly fail once two rounds of spades had gone by safely. The next play should be a spade, ruffed by the *king*, a diamond ruff, and a fourth spade, ruffed by the ten. East can overruff, but that is the only trick for the defence.

Always watch out for situations where a high ruff is safer than a low ruff.

Examples 38 and 39

One of the commonest and most useful manoeuvres in defence is the refusal to overruff the declarer in a situation such as this:

```
                 5 2
    K 10 4                     8 3
              A Q J 9 7 6
```

This is the trump suit and at some point in the play East leads a suit of which both declarer and West are void. South ruffs with the queen, and West, by declining to overruff, ensures a second trump trick for his side.

The same type of play is available to the declarer. Consider this deal:

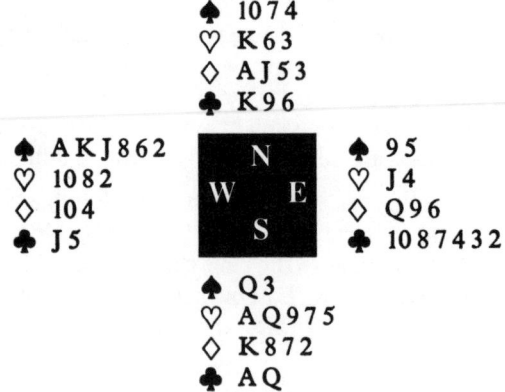

```
                 ♠ 10 7 4
                 ♡ K 6 3
                 ◇ A J 5 3
                 ♣ K 9 6

    ♠ A K J 8 6 2      N        ♠ 9 5
    ♡ 10 8 2       W       E    ♡ J 4
    ◇ 10 4             S        ◇ Q 9 6
    ♣ J 5                       ♣ 10 8 7 4 3 2

                 ♠ Q 3
                 ♡ A Q 9 7 5
                 ◇ K 8 7 2
                 ♣ A Q
```

South plays in four hearts and West, who has overcalled in spades, begins with king, ace and jack of this suit. Although the jack of spades is a master, East very properly ruffs with the jack of hearts and South overruffs with the queen. When he follows with the king and ace of hearts he is disappointed to find that the ten is still out against him. He can throw one diamond on the king of clubs, but sooner or later has to lose a trump and a diamond.

South made his mistake when he overruffed the jack of hearts. Instead, he should have discarded a diamond. Then he has no problem in drawing the trumps, cashing ace and queen of clubs, and discarding his other diamond loser on the king of clubs.

In a second example the hand that is shorter in trumps must discard a loser instead of overruffing.

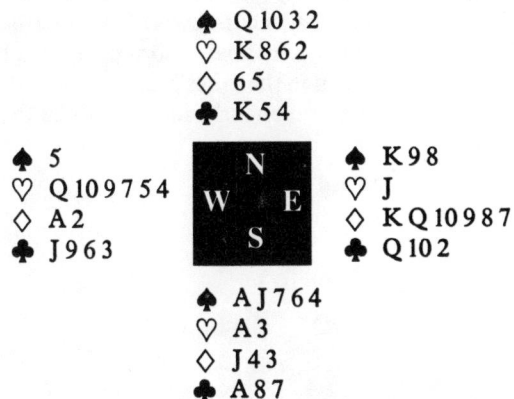

♠ Q 10 3 2
♡ K 8 6 2
◇ 6 5
♣ K 5 4

♠ 5
♡ Q 10 9 7 5 4
◇ A 2
♣ J 9 6 3

♠ K 9 8
♡ J
◇ K Q 10 9 8 7
♣ Q 10 2

♠ A J 7 6 4
♡ A 3
◇ J 4 3
♣ A 8 7

South plays in four spades after East has overcalled in diamonds. West leads the ace of diamonds and continues with the two to his partner's queen.

East is shrewd enough to realize (1) that his partner has no more diamonds, and (2) that if his partner can contribute a trump on the third round, he will force the ten of spades from dummy and establish a trick for the K 9 8. With this idea in mind, he returns the king of diamonds and West gallantly puts in his five of trumps.

It does not look bad to overruff—but if declarer does so, he will lose a trump trick to East and a club trick later on.

The right game is to discard the losing club from dummy instead of overruffing. Then the king of trumps can be picked up by a finesse and the third round of clubs can be ruffed on the table.

Example 40

We conclude this little study of safety plays with two coups that were considered the height of brilliancy when they were first described. (It would be pleasant, though somewhat naive, to suppose that they had their birth at the table rather than in the mind of an analyst.) By now, these plays are well understood, and once the idea is familiar they are not difficult to execute.

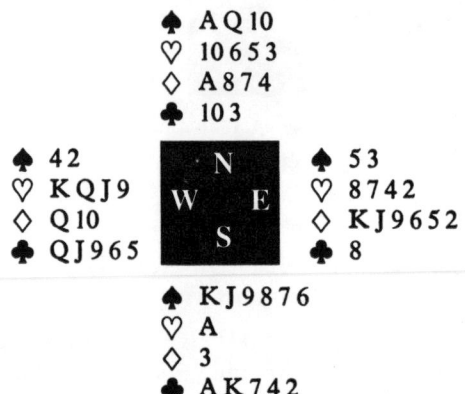

$$
\begin{array}{c}
\spadesuit \ A\,Q\,10 \\
\heartsuit \ 10\,6\,5\,3 \\
\diamondsuit \ A\,8\,7\,4 \\
\clubsuit \ 10\,3
\end{array}
$$

West:
- ♠ 42
- ♡ KQJ9
- ◇ Q10
- ♣ QJ965

East:
- ♠ 53
- ♡ 8742
- ◇ KJ9652
- ♣ 8

South:
- ♠ KJ9876
- ♡ A
- ◇ 3
- ♣ AK742

South plays in six spades and West leads the king of hearts. Obviously the clubs have to be developed, so declarer wins the heart and at once plays off ace and king of clubs. Bang! East ruffs and returns a trump. South suddenly finds that he has only two trumps in dummy and has three losers to ruff. It can't be done.

The safety play is to cash only one high club and to follow with a *low* club. The defenders take this and play a trump, but with K x x of clubs remaining, and still two trumps in dummy, declarer can comfortably ruff his two losers.

What would happen, do you think, if West were to strike a trump lead ?

Now ace and another club is not good enough, as West will win and play a second trump, leaving South with two club losers and only one spade in dummy.

However, as the cards lie, South can overcome the trump lead in another way. He cashes the ace of clubs, crosses to the ace of diamonds, and leads a second club from dummy. If East ruffs, he has no more trumps to lead; and if East lets this trick go, South wins and ruffs two clubs, losing the last one only.

Note the play of leading the second club *towards* the king, so that if East ruffs he will be ruffing a loser. It is an example of 'avoidance play' and is one of the commonest forms of safety play.

Example 41

Our final example is perhaps more a 'communication play' than a safety play. However, since it increases the declarer's chances by about 50%, it is a safety play in that sense.

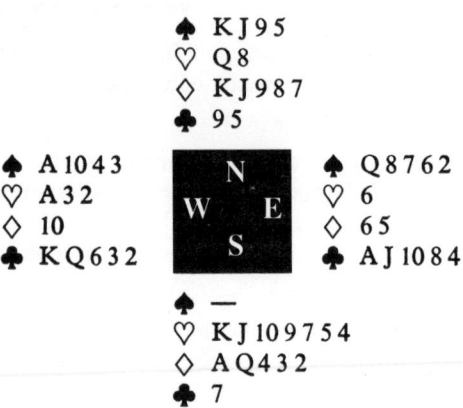

```
              ♠ K J 9 5
              ♡ Q 8
              ◇ K J 9 8 7
              ♣ 9 5
♠ A 10 4 3              ♠ Q 8 7 6 2
♡ A 3 2        N        ♡ 6
◇ 10       W     E      ◇ 6 5
♣ K Q 6 3 2    S        ♣ A J 10 8 4
              ♠ —
              ♡ K J 10 9 7 5 4
              ◇ A Q 4 3 2
              ♣ 7
```

After a competitive auction South plays in five hearts. West leads his singleton diamond, hoping to come in with the ace of hearts and give his partner the lead in either spades or clubs.

From declarer's point of view, the danger is obvious. The lead is surely a singleton, the ace of trumps has to be forced out, and the opponents can go from hand to hand in clubs.

Suppose South makes the obvious play of a trump at trick two. West will win and lead a club to his partner's ace. East, taking his cue from the fact that West has led a diamond rather than a suit bid by his side, will return a diamond for West to ruff.

Can declarer avert this sequence of plays ? Yes, by the brilliant stroke of leading the king of spades from dummy at trick two. He intends, if this is not covered by the ace, to discard his losing club. In that way he exchanges a club loser for a spade loser and meanwhile cuts the communications between the defending hands. The play is called the 'Scissors Coup'.